Sermons That Will Curl Your Hair

Pastor Albert Van Fisher

and Verdell Fisher

Unless otherwise noted, all Scripture quoted in this book are from The Authorized (King James) Version. Rights in the Authorized Version in the United Kingdom are vested in the Crown. Reproduced by permission of the Crown's patentee, Cambridge University Press.

Scripture (noted as TJB) taken from The Jerusalem Bible © 1966 by Darton Longman & Todd Ltd and Doubleday and Company Ltd.

Scripture (noted as NJKV) taken from the New King James Version®. Copyright © 1982 by Thomas Nelson. Used by permission. All rights reserved.

Scripture quotations marked (NIV) are taken from the Holy Bible, New International Version®, NIV®. Copyright © 1973, 1978, 1984, 2011 by Biblica, Inc.™ Used by permission of Zondervan. All rights reserved worldwide. www.zondervan.com The "NIV" and "New International Version" are trademarks registered in the United States Patent and Trademark Office by Biblica, Inc.™

Scripture marked (ESV) are from the ESV® Bible (The Holy Bible, English Standard Version®), copyright © 2001 by Crossway, a publishing ministry of Good News Publishers. Used by permission. All rights reserved.

Scripture quotations taken from the Amplified® Bible (AMP), Copyright© 2015 by The Lockman Foundation Used by permission. www.Lockman.org

Other quotations and sermons used in this book either consist of public domain works or are used by consent of those who submitted the sermons, poetry, etc.

Copyright © 2019 Pastor Albert Van Fisher and Verdell Fisher
All rights reserved. This book or any portion thereof may not be reproduced or used in any manner whatsoever without the express written permission of the publisher except for the use of brief quotations as allowed by the Fair Use Act.

Publisher: bylisabell
Radical Women
(DBA)
PO Box 782
Granbury, TX
76048
www.bylisabell.com

ISBN-10: 1-7325363-5-X
ISBN-13: 978-1-7325363-5-7

DEDICATION

This book is dedicated to my wife of 60 years. When I became ill, she promised to finish it for me, which made me very happy. I am a blessed man.
To my children Londell Fisher (deceased), Michelle Fisher, Ava Lanell Fisher Stevenson, Adrain Van Fisher Nolley.
To my grandchildren, Kevin Fisher, Candice White, Brittany Stevenson.
To my great-grandchildren, Morgan, Ryann, Ray'Jon, Mason and Ry'Lynn.
To my sister, Essie B. Johnson, the Salem Church family and the staff of Fisher's Beauty Salon.

Contents

Acknowledgments 7
Sermons by Pastor Albert Van Fisher 9
    Christmas Gladness 11
    Condemned for Misusing God-Given Privileges 17
    The Folks Who Are Different 21
    A New Song in the Air 27
    The Three What's of the Xian Life 31
    Walking on Earth in the Light of Heaven 35
    The Woman Who Did her Best 39
    The Gospel of an Eyewitness 43
    A Sunday Morning Hold-Up 49
    When My Mission Work Is Done 58
    Christ and the Common Man 62
    The Mailman's Mission 69
    Little Preachers and Big People 73
    Hot Lips and Cold Heart 76
    What Did You Come to Church For? 81
    Answering a Challenge 86
    Breaking Down Walls 91
    The Unique Position of the Gospel Preacher in This Disgraced Social Order ... 95
    Bring Me the Book 100
    The Presence of Christ in His Church 105
    The Devil is out to Get You 108

Do You Have Reservation? 115

Gideon 120

Tidbits to Make you Think, Smile or Laugh Out Loud 131

   Some Favorite Sayings 132

   Stories 132

   A Few Jokes 134

Sermons by Fellow Laborers (used by permission – bios included where provided) 137

   Unfounded Accusations 138

   The Immutability of the God of Indemnity 145

   Let Jesus Give you Rest* 150

   Sense and Common Sense in a World of nonsense 154

   If Loving You Is Wrong, I Don't Want To Be Right 165

   Men Ought Always Pray 170

   A Letter From the King 176

   Forever Being Guarded and Preserved by God 180

   Grasshopper Faith 184

   In A Nutshell 192

   Keep Moving—There is No Place to Park! 198

   Standing in the Safety Zone 201

   Favor and Leadership—an Overview 206

   What is the Anointing of the Holy Spirit? 212

   Whatsoever! 218

   ZION'S WAKE UP CALL 228

   Lads with his Mother's Blessings 231

   The Peace of God 236

   Double or Nothing 244

Trapped By Your Own Words 252

Pure Religion 262

The Crucifixion of King Self 266

Jesus' Last Teachings 274

Resolutions & Hints for the Church 278

  Baptist Church Officers and Staff Duties and Responsibilities 279

  Helpful Tools for the Church 291

    Jesus Christ Is... 293

    Jelly Bean Prayer 294

    You Blessed Me! 295

    "What Kind of Man Am I?" 297

    Let Freedom Ring 298

    Strategies for Improving Memory 299

    Are you Stepping Out for Christ Jesus? 301

    My Prayer to the Lord 303

    The Holy Alphabet 305

    Talk with God 306

    The Church Must Believe These Things 308

    Family Rules 310

Tributes to Pastor Fisher 311

  It Was Not Just About 312

  Tributes to Pastor Fisher 314

  Remembering my Neighbor and Friend 318

  Resolutions for Rev. Fisher 320

About the Author 331

Acknowledgments

Verdell Fisher continued the dream of this book. Without her diligence, the dream would have died in 2017. Thank you for picking up the dream and seeing it through to completion.

Rev. Leo Bromfield, Adrain Fisher Nolley, Michelle Fisher, Ava Fisher Stevenson, Mildred Sims, Kendle Fisher, Archie Prince, David Prince, Rev. Otis Darnell, David Ferrell, the late Glodine Long, the late Martha Jones, Theresa Smith, Rev. William Wood all played a role in the completion of this book. Thank you seems like inadequate words, but know that you have our sincere gratitude.

To Lisa Bell and staff (DBA Radical Women) thank you for the hours of typing, compilation, editing and work put in this project. May God bless your efforts and continue using you to further His Kingdom.

"Being confident of this very thing, that he which hath begun a good work in you will perform it until the day of Jesus Christ." Philippians 1:6 (KJV)

Sermons by Pastor Albert Van Fisher

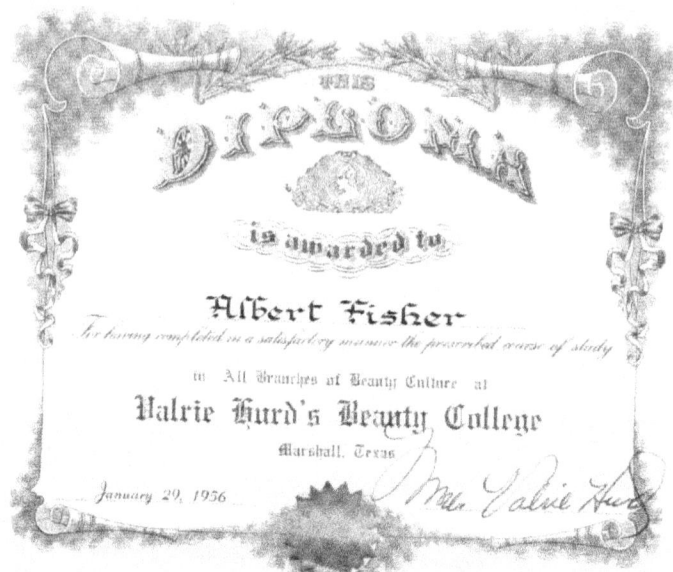

Dr. Martin Luther King, Jr., Memorial Prayer Breakfast

In Memoriam

* * * * *

Honoring the Memory of

Dr. A.V. Fisher
1933-2017

Awarded On This The 15th Day Of January, In The Year Of Our Lord 2018

Reverend Julius L. Jackson, Jr. & Reverend Raymond Oliver, Coordinators

Christmas Gladness

"Fear not; for behold I bring you good tiding of great joy."
Luke 2:10

This is good news and we can fling it to every wind that blows, until December's chill is made as pleasant anthems resound across the wintry lands and echo where the scented flowers bloom.

Christ knows no East, no West, no North, no South, no caste and no prescribed rank. In him we are one fellowship linked to the brother whose gentle constraint woos the most unwilling. We gain today the meaning of the past, assured the love of our Father and the union of our present life with life eternal.

Cottage and mansion, high and lowly, rich and poor, can jubilate together. We can stop awhile and think of the children of the slum, of our own children, of the friends that love us, of the many trials through which we have come. We can bury our dislikes and enmities and greet our friends and foes and open our glad heart's door to let the Christ child in.

The Christmas sunshine- the bursting forth of the heavenly dayspring upon earth's darkness. This is the deeper significance of the Christmas joy message. It means the bursting of the tides of heavenly gladness through the crust of the earth.

How thoroughly typical of this was the effulgence that illumined the sky near Bethlehem on that glad night of nights and how sublime is the word picture painted by Luke.

How the light flowing from the dayspring has penetrated the dark places of this old earth and illumined them with joy! How true it is that Christ came "to give light to them that sit in darkness".

That radiance shines upon lives steeped in guilt and the shadows of hopeless regret are scattered and penitent souls find joy in pardon and hope replaces despair.

That sunlight falls upon the dark places of earthly experiences and even the valley of the shadow of death loses its power to arouse fear.

Like a powerful searchlight, it shines into the unfathomed future and life and immortality are brought to light. Surely Christ's coming means above all things else, eternal sunshine for sin-darkened souls.

The World's Sweetest Joy

In his human birth Jesus became a part of the world's sweetest and most primitive joy-the joy that awakens when it is said, "a child is born." Only brutalized or perverted natures do not feel that thrill.

In the mansion, in the great city, or in the lonely cabin out on the rim of the world, this joy is the same. Poverty and wealth have nothing to do with it. Bed of straw on manger floor, or queen's couch canopied with silk and gold, it is all the same.

The birth song is the note of the world's generic happiness that in humankind, is one with the joy of a bird that flutters and sings above her nestlings and with that yet more primitive hear-quiver that runs through all lower life with the shooting of a seed and the opening of a flower.

So Jesus entered the stream of human joy, not halfway down its course but at its fountain head. Evermore, since Bethlehem, young mothers will think of him when they first feel the touch of soft baby fingers upon their breasts and the strong man will think of him when with deep joy and pride he first lifts up a little child and says, "This is my son."

The World's Greatest Xmas Gift

On Christmas morning we say, "Xmas Gift" instead of "Merry Christmas." A present is claimed from the one who is thus caught. "Xmas Gift" says Daughter. House to house visitor. "Xmas Gift" ole masta" says the slave. "Ise been faithful to you all dis year."

Can we come this Xmas season with the same please to our Master? Can we say truthfully, "I have served you faithfully all this year? A little extra gift to close the year." We are a privileged class to ask this. For we are told by Christ to "Ask, and it shall be given you, seek and you shall find. Knock and it shall be opened unto you. For EVERY ONE that asketh, receiveth and he that seeketh findeth; and to him that knocketh, it shall be opened." Luke 11:9-10

So gladly will he give to each one, with his salvation, wisdom, patience, gentleness, power, hope, joy and love.

He likes to throw in the extras.

When Jesus came into the world, the religion of the then civilized world, the Roman Empire, was a religion of fear which was based on the idea that the gods were powerful and dangerous, and that it was necessary to placate the wrath of these gods, or win their favor; and that was the general view of the common people all around the globe.

There might have been philosophers who held a different view but that was the common opinion everywhere-worship or sacrifice, penance or pilgrimage, or payment to win the favor of the gods. They were powerful gods; they were liable to angry gods and were dangerous gods. The gods are the ideals of the people. Religion was reverence for power inspired by fear.

Government was reverence for power inspired by fear. The government of Rome was an absolute despotism. Men obeyed because the Emperor had power to compel obedience. Men feared the law and that government was carried on for the benefit of the gods.

The same spirit animated industry. Industry was a kind of grab game. It is somewhat so now but it was so altogether then. Industry was compelled by fear.

But when Jesus appeared on the scene, he said, "You are making a great mistake. Religion is not to be feared. The power of your government is not to be feared. The power of your industry is not to be feared. It is something else very different."

Curiously enough, Jesus never said anything particularly about the power of God; he never said anything particularly about the wisdom of God; if he did it was incidental. What he laid stress on was this: Not that God has power and wisdom but that God was love. He said "you fathers give good gifts to your children: believe that your Father in heaven will give good gifts to you. You forgive your trespassers; believe that your Father in heaven will forgive your trespasses."

At a time when men did not believe that God forgave at all unless his forgiveness were bought, Christ said, "That is not true: You fathers forgive and so believe your Father forgives you.

Nothing is too little for him; nothing that interests you fails to interest him. Don't think you have to buy his forgiveness. You don't need to offer sacrifice. Christ never even suggested that sacrifice must be offered. For God is love, not merely tender love but love with a wonderful amount of faith and confidence in man.

The World Needs Christ

The people need Christ. They have their share of sin, suffering and sorrow. We deeply need the grace, consolations and strengthening of the gospel. We are capable of Christ without the intellectual distinction of the Magi or the social eminence of Herod. We have the essential greatness of soul which renders us capable of Christ and his greatest gifts. We rejoice in Christ.

"The shepherds returned, glorifying and praising God for all the things that they had heard and seen." From that day to this a new glory has shone on all common scenes. A new joy has filled the common heart that has been opened to the Prince of Peace, the Saviour of the world.

Condemned for Misusing God-Given Privileges

"The men of Nineveh shall rise up in the judgement with this generation and shall condemn it." Luke 11:32

Jesus and his apostles again and again called attention to the fact that many persons were condemned, not for some crime but because they were rejecting God-given gospel privileges.

"And whosoever shall not receive you, nor hear your words, when ye depart out of that house or city, shake the dust off your feet. Verily I say unto you, it shall be more tolerable for the land of Sodom and Gomorrah in the day of judgement than for that city." Matthew 10:14-15

Jesus in particular pressed home upon us some very great truths about the sin of misusing great gospel privileges. Let us examine a few of them.

God gives sufficient light to every man to lead him to the perfect light, if he would follow it.

Jesus was the true light: "There was the true light, even that which lighteth every man, coming into the world." John 1:9 "And this is the judgement, that the light is come into the world, and men loved the darkness rather than the light; for their works were evil." John 3:19

Paul makes this statement about the heathen:

"Because that which is known of God is manifest in them; for God manifested it unto them. For the invisible things of him since the creation of the world are clearly seen, being perceived through the things that are made, even his everlasting power and divinity; that they may be without excuse." Romans 1:19-20

In fact, God has written some very great moral truths deep in every man's soul, savage or civilized, so the better life, no matter where he goes.

But God gives greater light to some persons than to others.

Jesus said that if Sodom and Gomorrah had had the privileges which he gave to some of the cities in Galilee they would have repented long since.

"And thou, Capernaum which art exalted unto heaven, shall be brought down to hell: for if the mighty works which have been done is holy. All of their holiness they derive from him and it is complete in him."

Our peace and comfort is complete in Christ.

He is our peace. His word is the word of peace. The legacy he has bequeathed his church, is his peace. His peace dwells in us richly and we possess and comfort through believing in him. "Peace I leave with you, my peace I give unto you, not as the World giveth, give I unto you. Let not your heart be troubled, neither let it be afraid." John 14:27.

Our services are complete in him.

We serve by the aids of his grace. Our services are only acceptable as they ascend through the medium of his merits and are rendered holy by priestly intercessions to his glory. "And another angel came and stood at the altar having a golden censor and there was given him much incense that he should offer it with the prayers of all the saints upon the golden altar which was before the throne."

"And the smoke of the incense which came with the prayers of the saints ascended up before God out of the angel's hand." Revelation 8:3-4

They must all be done in his name and to his glory. "Whatsoever ye do, do all in the name of the lord Jesus.

Our Triumph Over Our Spiritual Adversaries is Complete in Christ

He supplies us with invincible armor.

1. Breast plate of righteousness.
2. The girdle of truth.
3. The sword of the spirit etc.

"We are more than conquerors through him that loved us." Romans 8:37

"We can do all things through Christ who strengtheneth us." Philippians 4:13

Our Tranquility and happiness in Death are Complete in Christ

His death has hallowed the narrow limits of the grave. His body gave to the sweet smelling savor and irradiated it with hope and glory. Death is now the chartered friend of the Christian. "To die is gain." "Blessed are the dead who die in the Lord." Yes, sayeth the spirit, they rest from their labor.

Our Resurrection and Eternal Glory are Complete in Christ

"I am the resurrection and the life."

He became the first fruits of them that slept. He will

change our vile bodies. He will confess the righteous and give them the crown of life that fadeth not away.

He will receive them to his glory. Welcome them to his kingdom and give unto them eternal life.

All that is sacred and precious in the interests of the Christian whether for life or death or eternity is complete in Jesus Christ.

This completeness must be personally realized by the experience of his grace in our hearts. We must be in Christ and Christ in us, the hope of glory.

The Folks Who Are Different

"What do ye more than others?" Matthew 5:47

This is an arresting and searching question. It is evident that Jesus expects his followers to be vastly different from those about them.

He came at a cost to himself beyond our powers to understand. To do something for us that we cannot do for ourselves. It was for the joy that was set before him, a joy measured in transformed lives that he endured the cross, despising the shame.

Just what difference then has his coming made in your life and mine? What is there about us as professing Christians that is special? If there is nothing, then our Christianity is a futile something, a disappointment to ourselves and a far keener disappointment to him whom we claim as our Lord and Master.

Assuming then that our Christianity is genuine, what is there distinctive about us? Perhaps we can get a clearer answer to this question by looking at the early church. Often we can see what is far off better than we can see what is near. As we turn the pages of the New Testament, what do we find that the Christian possessed that his unbelieving neighbor did not possess?

These early Christians specialized in brotherliness.

The Christian of the first century out loved his pagan neighbor. He was far more brotherly. There was a breadth and depth about his love that was beautifully distinctive.

These early Christians specialized in love one for another. They had been so taught by their Master. How, according to Jesus, are we to distinguish one who is a Christian from one who is not?

"By this shall all men know that ye are my disciples." If...if, what if you belong to a certain denomination? If you belong to a certain class or niche in the upper crust? No, if you are popular because of your ability to mix in with the crowds? No, not that but this, "If ye have love one to another."

It was by one Christian thus loving his fellow Christian that these early saints made perhaps their most profound impression upon the world of their day. "How these Christians love each other!" men exclaimed in awe and wonder. And because these pagans longed to love and to be loved, they were drawn into those Christian groups that Paul called "colonies of heaven." To this day there is nothing so winsome as an atmosphere made warm and vital by the presence of those who really love each other.

Not only did these followers of Jesus love one another, not only did they love the brotherhood but they loved those outside the brotherhood. They loved strangers, foreigners and outsiders. If our world is divided today by deep and wide chasms that ancient world was divided by chasms that were deeper and wider still.

Yet there was no chasm that separated people in that day that Christianity did not bridge. It bridged the chasm between God and man, between man and man, race and race. It bridges the chasm between people who were respectable and those who were outcast. It gave to social bodies and slaves healing for their wounded self-respect by bringing them into the brotherhood. These early Christians were possessed of an eager interest in every human soul. They not only loved on another but they loved strangers and outsiders.

Finally, these disciples of Jesus not only loved on another, not only did they love strangers and foreigners but they loved their enemies. That is something that the man of the world not only does not do but does not even desire to do.

But these Christians did love their enemies. Really Christians still do. If they do not, they are not Christians. Christian love, however, does not mean fondness for or delight in one's enemies, they are not the ones that we choose as our house guests. We would hardly take a snake in our bosom knowing it to be a snake.

But we love our enemies when we exercise toward them an active and sacrificial good will. Such love Jesus taught, such love Jesus practiced. "Bless them that curse you...Pray for them that despitefully use you and persecute you" is his exacting word. So he himself did. He did it even as he hung on the cross. Here he threw about the shoulders of his murderers the sheltering folds of this protecting prayer: "Father forgive them for they know not what they do."

Here is another scene. A brilliant and gifted young man, Stephen by name, has become a follower of the Christ. He proclaims his faith with irresistible power. His foes, being unable to answer him with words, resort to stones. They drag him outside the city and mob him. There is no effort at justice of fair play. He is gone to death without even a mock trial. How does he meet this terrible ordeal? He meets it in the Spirit of his Master.

When we hear him pray this prayer, "Lord, lay not this sin to their charge" we know that we are in the presence of a Christian. These early Christians specialized in brotherliness in that they loved one another, they loved outsiders, and they loved even their enemies. Such love must be practiced by the Christians of this day if we lay claim to the Christianity taught by Christ.

Dare to Live Life the Hard Way

These early Christians specialized in a fine gallantry that made them dare to live life the hard way. They went out, not simply to follow Christ but to reproduce him. Thus they sought to make him King over all that pagan world. Their adventure was costly. Their Master had made this fact plain to them from the beginning. They had become followers of Jesus knowing that such would be the case. They knew that they would have to pay much, even their very all.

Jesus also makes this plain to us. He declares that there is a wide gate and an easy way but that this leads to death. If we are bent on life we must enter by the narrow gate and travel the hard way. It was so hard for Jesus himself that it involved the cross. He never promised that it would be easier for us. He said, "If any man will come after me, let him deny himself and take up his cross and follow me."

At the very door of entrance to life there stands a cross upon which we must die to self. This dying to self is often as painful as physical death. But there is no beginning of the Christian life without this dying to self. There is no continuing it without this daily dying to ourselves. There simply is no cheap and easy way to be a Christian.

If you will turn the pages of your Bible with this in mind you will be impressed how little God seems to for the ease and comfort of his saints.

Take those men of the Old Testament who were most loyal to him and who became his closest friends. These heroic souls were willing to dare any danger, brave any death rather than prove disloyal. What response did God make to them? Did he see that no rude wind blew upon them? Did he shelter and coddle them? Here is the answer.

"They were stoned, they were sawn asunder, were tempted, were slain with the sword. They wandered about in sheepskins and goatskins. Being destitute, afflicted, tormented they wandered in deserts and in mountains and in dens and caves of the earth."

What is perhaps stranger still, this indifference on the part of God the ease and comfort of his saints was shared by these saints themselves. Notice in the New Testament how the followers of Jesus prayed when they found themselves with their backs to the wall. Their prayers were never for escape. Those who prayed only for escape were never followers of Christ.

Here are two revolutionaries who died at the side of Jesus. One of them is a truly great soul.

After he has taken the part of Jesus against those who are doing him to death, he prays this payer for himself. "Lord remember me when thou comest into thy Kingdom." He wants deliverance not from where he is, even though he is suffering the pangs of hell. He rather seeks deliverance from what he is.

But the lesser revolutionary does not mind being what he is. He only hates being where he is. Therefore, he prays this prayer, "If thou be the Son of God, save thyself and us."

But listen to the saints as they pray "And now Lord, behold their threatenings." Who is doing the threatening? The very same men who had crucified their Master. They know therefore that these are not vain threats. Their danger is real. For what then do they pray? They do not ask for escape.

This is their prayer, "Grant unto thy servants that with all boldness they may speak thy word." They do not ask for an easy way. They ask rather that they may see their hard way through with honor.

Here is Paul writing a letter from prison in Rome. By and by he comes to the matter of prayer.

A New Song in the Air

"God so loved the World that he gave..." John 3:16

There's a new song in the air. The old song was sung with jubilation and the happiness that accompanies an erstwhile freedom from the shackles of physical bondage and slavery. It was the song of Miriam, the sister of Moses. All the people joined her in:

"The Lord hath triumphed gloriously, the hose and his rider hath he thrown into the sea. The Lord is my strength and song and he is become my salvation. He is my God, my father's God and I will exalt him. The Lord is his name. Pharaoh's chariots and his host hath he cast into the sea. His chosen captains also are drowned in the red sea. The Depths have covered them. They sank into the bottom as a stone. Thy right hand, O Lord, is become glorious in power. Thy right hand, O Lord, hath dashed in pieces the enemy."

This was the old song of triumph over the enemy. But the new song in the air is one that strikes the cord of love in the heart of humanity for our enemies as well as our friends.

The title of this song is "Love." "For God so loved the world that he GAVE..."

The new song in the air embraces the Xmas spirit. It is a triune symphony of spiritual harmonies. The whole world harmonizing at the same time.

One Strain of This Song in the Air is its Gently Penetrating Charm

All the world is drawn under its spell. The Christmas season is marked by special manifestations of human kindness. It is the season of regenerated feelings. Men turn for once in the year from thoughts of self to others. We ask ourselves the question, "What shall be my gift to him or to her?"

Without the pressure of organized religion, cities and towns and hamlets are thinking of their poor and needy and are bombarding citizens with mercy calls. The mails are choked with sincere greetings of the season and the air resounds with the words, "Merry Christmas."

Whence comes this spirit of goodwill? It is the annually renewed echo of the angelic song above the windswept hills of Bethlehem. And the heart of that song is that "God so loved that he GAVE."

An influence emanates from that song like the glow from some kindly light whose radiance is annually heightened at the Christmas season. When then the mystic charm of the song? From God himself incarnate in the flesh. Only God could have given us Christmas. It is at this point that Paul cries out, *"Thanks be unto God for his unspeakable gift."* 2 Corinthians 9:15

Because of its Origin

From everlasting to everlasting. Always was, always

will bel. Alpha and Omega. Fills all space.

Because of its Worth

All nature is impoverished to set him forth. He is the pearl of great price. Bright and morning Star. Son of righteousness. The bread of life. He is the life as well as the light of the world. He is the fountain of all existence. He is the great supreme good of all his creatures. He is earth's benefactor and heaven's Lord and glory.

Because of its Benefits

It is the gift in which all blessings are comprehended. It is the gift of gifts. It is the gifts.

It is the basis and medium of all our mercies including life, light, pardon, peace, adoption, holiness and eternal glory.

Because of its Durability

Everything on earth is frail and unstable. But this gift is abiding, changeless and eternal. He is the same "today, yesterday and forever."

A Second Strain of This Song is its Heavenly Chord of Unselfishness

What season of the year is so filled with unselfishness? The season is charged with goodwill. As one is prompted to whistle a tune running through his mind, so are men these days prompted to express their thoughtfulness of others. Life is an unfinished symphony. There is always something near trying to lay hands upon us. There is something seeking to make itself felt and heard. Here and there a glint of the eternal will soon break through. The face of the Christ Child will be seen.

The Three What's of the Xian Life

"The eye of your understanding being enlightened; that ye may know WHAT is the hope of his calling, and WHAT the riches of the glory of his inheritance of the saints, and WHAT is the exceeding greatness of his power to us-ward who believe, according to the working of his mighty power." Ephesians 1:18-19

- The source of spiritual enlightenment is God.
- The agency is that of the Holy Spirit.
- The end is the knowing, owning and glorifying God.
- That Ye May Know What is the Hope

The child of God is already in possession of forgiveness, acceptance in Christ, adoption into the divine family but there is much more to follow. The hope of the Christian is:

A living hope. 1 Peter 1:3 *"Blessed be the God and Father of our lord Jesus Christ, which according to his abundant mercy hath begotten us again unto a lively hope by the resurrection of Jesus Christ from the dead."* The hope of life. Abundant life. Eternal life.

A sure hope. Hebrew 6:19 *"Which hope we have as an anchor of the soul, both sure and steadfast and which entereth into that within the vail."* The hope of the hypocrite shall perish and that of the ungodly shall be cut off. The believer cannot fail unless the divine veracity, the precious blood of Jesus, the intercession of Christ- fails.

A blessed hope. Titus 2:13 *"Looking for that blessed hope and the glorious appearing of the great God and our Saviour Jesus Christ."*

A glorious hope. Colossians 1:29 *"To whom God would make known what is the riches of the glory of the mystery among the Gentiles; which is Christ in you, the hope of glory."* Glorious-that which is splendid, that which is great, that which is rich and magnificent.

A heavenly hope. It is the hope of heaven.

The hope of his calling. 2 Peter 1:10 *"Brethren, give diligence to make your calling and election sure."* If ye do these things, ye shall never fail.

What is the Riches of the Glory?

How vast are the riches of God.

The World is His. Psalms 50:12 *"If I were hungry I would not tell thee; for the world is mine and the fullness thereof."*

Heaven is His. Angels, Principalities, Mansions, Thrones

He is rich in himself. Rich in knowledge, wisdom, grace, love, power.

His Saints are his greatest riches. For these the earth was made, heaven prepared, God's wisdom, love, mercy, grace expended. Saints are God's specialty. Every saint is bequeathed to God by himself in an everlasting Covenant. Daniel 7:18 *"But the saints of the most High shall take the Kingdom and possess the Kingdom forever, even forever and ever."*

What is the Greatness of His Power?

It is the same power that raised Christ from the dead therefore is:

Divine-not angelic, nor arch-angelic. Much less human.

It is Resurrection power. Power to give life to the dead.

It is irresistible power. No seal, no chief priest, no demons could hold him.

It is glorious power. It reflected great honor upon God and brought great dismay to his enemies.

It is everlasting power. Christ being raised, dieth no more. Death has no more dominion over him.

It is lifting power. Ephesians 1:21 *"Far above all principality and power and might and dominion and every name that is named, not only in this world but also in that world which is to come."*

The knowledge is only for his saints, His holy ones.

The exceeding greatness of God's power is revealed only to those who believe. *"He that cometh to God must believe that he is and that he's a rewarder of them that diligently seek him."* Hebrews 11:6

The Divinity of Jesus

Absolute immutability is one of the essential attributes of God. Yet it is obviously ascribed to Christ.

The Security of His Cause

All he is and has, stand pledged for the security and final triumph of his cause. It rests on his immutability. If he cannot change, the results are sure and certain.

The Comfort of Believers

In seasons of darkness, temptation, weakness, affliction, death, Jesus the source of all grace and consolation, is the same "yesterday, today and forever."

Walking on Earth in the Light of Heaven

"O house of Jacob, come and let us walk in the light of the Lord." Isaiah 2:5 *"But if we walk in the light, as He is in the light, we have fellowship one with another."* 1 John 1:7

Here is an invitation to:

A Heavenly Walk

This walk begins in conversion; no longer walking in darkness. *"If we say we have fellowship with him and walk in darkness, we lie and do not tell the truth."* 1 John 1:6

By reconciliation; no longer aliens, rebels. *"How two walk together except they be agreed?"* Amos

Obedience; following the guide, or consulting the guide book.

Progress; step by step; repentance, faith, love, etc.

Walk in Heavenly Light

It is a divine light, "light of the Lord." Isaiah "God is light." John 1:5

It is true light. "The true light now shineth."

It is increasing light. "Shineth more and more."

It is satisfying light. It satisfies the mind, conscience, heart.

With Heavenly Companions

Fellowship with the Father, as children we share his favor, His love, care and house.

Fellowship with the son. He whose wisdom is unerring, whose power is unlimited, whose love is infinite; took upon him our nature, we are members of his body.

Fellowship with one another; a community of natures, views, feelings, joy, sorrow and interests. Fellowship with God, with Jesus, with God's children is one and inseparable.

For Heavenly Cleansing

It is a complete cleansing. All sin.

It is a present cleansing. Not SHALL, but cleanseth NOW.

It is a certain cleansing. "Though your sins be as scarlet, (with healing in his wings) who have suffered in this world. Then again, he will descend in a cloud for judgement and all the holy angels with him."

The judgement over, he will arise as the light of the world. For God is light. And we will walk in that light.

"They need no candle, neither light of the sun, for the Lord God giveth them light and they shall reign forever and ever." Revelations 22:5

Sunrise
"For behold, the day cometh that shall burn as an oven and all the proud, yea and all that do wickedly shall be stubble. And the day that cometh shall burn them up, saith the Lord of hosts,

that it shall leave them neither root nor branch. But unto you that fear my name shall the Sun of righteousness arise with healing in his wings and ye shall go forth and grow up as calves of the stall." Malachi 4:1-2

A Contrast. But unto you.
All that do wickedly.

This includes all the impenitent and unregenerate in all ages whose end is to be burned.

"But unto you that fear my name. Then they that feared the Lord spake often." Ch. 3:16 -to one another." This promise is to the God fearing in all ages. Daniel, David, Hebrew children, Paul, Peter, etc. To fear his name is to fear to offend.

A Comparison
"Sun of righteousness." Jesus is like the sun in his oneness. In the universes there is infinite variety.

Many rivers, many stars, many cloud but only one sun. Only one Christ. "There is no other name under heaven whereby men may be saved. They saw no man save Jesus only." Matthew 17:8

His Centralness. Just as the worlds are linked to the sun by gravitation, so are we linked to Jesus by love.

His Light. The sun is the source of physical light. So Jesus is the source of all spiritual light.

The sun is the great quickener. "I am the way, the truth and the lift." The blade of grass, grain of corn, small flower seed are all brought to life by the sun.

He is the joy giver. His gladness. *"Weeping may endure for a night but joy cometh in the morning."* Psalms 30:5

Impartialness. The sun makes no selection. Neither does Jesus. "Whosoever,"

A Consummation. Sun Rise.
Jesus arose in the scriptures through the prophecies and promises.

He shall arise when he comes in His glory. First he will descend and come to the aid of his children.

The Woman Who Did her Best

"She hath done what she could." Mark 14:8

The introduction of feminine character and life into early Christianity gave a force and fervency to the whole movement. The church is the appointed instrument of God in the evangelization of the world and woman has ever been and still is the heart of the church as she is the conscience of the race. She is the numerical majority of the church.

This Woman Wanted to do Something

The woman who lives in this great world of opportunity and need and does nothing will have no need to shudder when she at last stands in the presence of Jesus. Mary was not satisfied to live and die on flowery beds of ease while there was so much work to be done in the Kingdom.

The great drawbacks in our churches today are not found in people who are incompetent but those who are unwilling to do anything. They are too ornery to do anything themselves and just ornery enough to try to keep others from doing anything.

She Was Willing to do What She Could. Nabal.

Abagail, to save her husband and his property hastens to the foot of the hill. No sword, no spear but her own beauty and willingness. When David sees her kneeling at the base of the crag, he cries: Halt! Halt!

And the caverns echo the cry: Halt! Halt! Abagail is the conqueror. One woman in the right, mightier than four hundred men in the wrong. A hurricane stopped at the sight of a water-lily. A dew-drop dashed back Niagara Falls.

By her prowess and tact she had saved her husband and her home and put before all ages an illustrious specimen of what a woman can do if she is Godly, prudent, willing and self-sacrificing. Enough they can do important things in the church community.

There were doubtless many things which Mary could not do. She was not fitted for speech-making as so many of our modern women. Possibly she could not have presided over a meeting. But she could slip in quietly and prepare the feet of Jesus for his burial. This she could do and was willing to do. Without anybody telling her to do so.

There are many people like Mary in and about our churches. He is with them as their head, to direct and superintend. As their friend, to supply all their wants out of his boundless goodness. As their prophet, to instruct. As the Mediator, to be the medium of access to God. And as their king, to sway over them the mild and gracious scepter of his grace.

The Evidence of God's Presence
- External splendor, great wealth, a multitude of members are not evidences.
- Scriptural doctrine is an evidence
- When his word is the standard, when the scriptures are honored and the truth held, as it is in Jesus.
- Purity of ordinances is an evidence.
- Where there are no inventions of men. Where Christ's ordinances are rightly administered. None invented, none alloyed, none abandoned.
- Brotherly love is an evidence.
- God is love. Where his spirit is, there will be love. Love to all the brethren, love unfeigned. *"By this shall all men know ye are my disciples."*

When divine changes are produced by the power of the Gospel.

Careless souls aroused, sinners convinced, mourners comforted and believers edified.

When we endure the reproach of the cross.

It is a bad sign when the world smiles and speaks well of the church. The World is at enmity with the church. *"We must through much tribulation enter the kingdom."* Acts 14:22

"Know ye not that the friendship of the world is enmity with God? Whosoever therefore will be a friend of the world, is the enemy of God." James 4:4

"If ye were of the world, the world would love his own, but because ye are not of the world but I have chosen you out of the

world, therefore the world hateth you." John 15:19

The influence of the presence of God in the church shall produce upon those who are without.

"We will go with you." This resolution implies:
Dissatisfaction with their present condition.

Unhappy, without peace and without hope. Have found all to be vain and empty and insufficient. Every resource has been a broken cistern.

Earnest desire to be united with God's people.

"We will go with you. Not merely say as you say but do as you do. We will go with you to the house of God. I was glad when they said unto me, let us go into the house of the lord." Psalms 122:1

We will go with you to the throne of grace (prayer meeting). We will go with you to the cross.

As soldiers of the cross, we will go with you to the field of conflict, death and eternal glory. The Saints already await our coming.

Moses to Hobab: *"Come thou with us and we will do thee good, for the Lord has spoken good concerning Israel."* Numbers 10:29

The Gospel of an Eyewitness

"THEY COULD NOT MAKE HIM HUSH"

Nothing has so much weight with a judge or a jury as an eye witness. Enough eye witnesses can win any case regardless of how difficult it is. The voice of experience, the testimony of fact, cannot be repudiated easily.

JESUS RESTORED THE BLIND HIS SIGHT

A Great Christian was once asked the question, "How do you know that you have been saved?" He answered, "I was there when it happened." In the ninth chapter of John, we hear a man giving such a testimony. He had never seen a smile or a tear. He was born blind. He had been blind all of his life but Jesus came along one day and gave him his sight. When he was asked about it, he said, "I don't know all about Jesus, but this I know...I was blind; now I see." (C.F. The blessedness of sight.)

This experience is called conversion. It happens to different people in different ways. It is the most radical change that can come to a man. In conversion one passes from death unto life and from blindness to glorious sight. In conversion, all things become new. In conversion, life is made different and one's heart is filled with hope. So you hear me. Why?

The experience of conversion came to Paul in a blinding light when the power of Christ knocked him to the ground. It came to Lydia in the quietness at a riverside prayer meeting. It came to me in a little country church revival. It happens to different people in different ways but in everyone a great change is wrought. Doors are locked and bars on the door but you can't lock out Death. (Help me now).

Paul cried out, "I have passed from death unto life. This man declared, "...I was blind, now I see."

I thank God for Jesus. There never was a man with such a compassionate heart and with such divine power as Jesus. When men were in distress, Jesus was disturbed. Death, storm, "But not Prayer." A person always moved the heart of Jesus.

Jesus is all things to all men.

    To the hungry, He is the bread of life.

    To the thirsty, He is the living water.

    To the lost, He is the way.

    To the dead, He is life.

    To the blind, He is the light of the world.

Light unto our feet a lamp unto our path. Jesus is all things to all men. Here in the city of Jerusalem at the feast of the tabernacles, our Lord met this unnamed man who had been blind from his birth. He had felt his way through life from his birth. He was grown now. He had never seen the light of day.

Blindness is called the heaviest bodily cross. He had been cut off from most of the highest enjoyments of life.

He had never seen the faces of his parents, or any of his kindred and friends. He had never seen a raindrop or a snowflake. He had never seen a flower or a tree. He had never seen a mountain or a river, or a bird, or a bee. He was born blind. The man never seen the sun or moon or stars. He had never seen this beautiful world in which he was living. He had never seen a single crumb of bread that he had eaten. He had never seen a drop of water that he had drunk. He was born blind.

WHAT HAPPENED?

Jesus passed his way. "Jesus said that the man was born blind so that the works of God should be made manifested in him." (John 9:3) Jesus gave the man his sight. A great controversy here.

As a rule, Jesus healed men on the basis of faith alone but here Jesus uses a means. He anointed the man's eye with clay and "sent" him to the pool of Siloam to wash. "Made clay out of dirt."

The method is always up to the Lord. He can heal with doctors and medicine, or he can heal without them. The method is up to Him...HELP ME.

The man received his sight. He washed and came seeing and the critics came out. His neighbors couldn't understand it. They all disputed he was healed. He was interviewed again and again and each time he gave but one answer and that was: "...One thing I know, that, whereas I was blind, now I see." They could not make him HUSH!

This man did not argue with them. He simply stated

a fact. He startled their minds, enraged their fury and held them at bay on his one point. He won the debate, yet he had never studied debating. He was just a plain eye witness for the Lord.

If I could read, he would say. He could sing truthfully in the words of John Newton:

"Amazing grace, how sweet the sound that saved a wretch like me! I once was lost but now I'm found, was blind but now I see.

"Yea, when this flesh and mortal life shall cease, I shall possess within the veil. A life of joy and peace."

When Jesus saw the man born blind, His compassion was stirred and he said, *"I must work the works of him that sent me, while it is day; the night cometh when no man can work."* John 9:4

Jesus warns us here that the curtain of our lives will soon fail and our opportunities will be over forever. We must use our opportunities.

It is said of Michelangelo that while he worked on the statue of David he slept in his clothes, kept some food at his side and ate a bite from time to time.

It is said of John Milton, the blind poet, he arose at four o'clock in the morning to write his poetry when his mind was fresh.

It is said of John Wesley that when the churches were closed to him, he went out in the cemetery and used his father's tombstone for a pulpit. Wesley was zealous for the Lord.

Just a few more years now, and the night will come when we can work no more.

"WE'LL JUST HAVE TO PUT IT IN THE HANDS OF THE LORD."

The poet put it this way: "*A few more years shall roll, A few more seasons come, And we shall be with those that rest, Asleep within the tomb. Then, O, my Lord, prepare my soul for that great day; O, wash me in that precious blood, And take my sins away.*"

The neighbors, and Pharisees, and Sadducees all seemed to have turned against the man. They cast him out of the synagogue. They reviled him. But with the Lord on your side, you can stand almost anything.

There are so many times when I don't know what I would do without the Lord.

John G. Paton and his Christian Wife were sent as missionaries to the New Hebrides. A year later, a baby was born to them but it cost Ms. Paton her life. The lonely missionary dug her grave himself and buried her. Two days later, the baby died and he dug its graved and buried it by the side of its mother.

Later he said, "In that wild land, the only consolation I had was in Christ. Had it not been for the Lord, I would have died myself."

There are some things that you cannot stand without Christ. With Christ all things are possible. If Christ is for you, He is more than all the world against you.

When they put the man out of the synagogue, Jesus heard about it and rushed to his rescue. When the world defeats us and trouble comes and we need a friend, Jesus is near just when you need Him most.

TRUST IN THE LORD.

A certain mother went to school each afternoon to bring her little girl home. One day the driveway was covered with ice and the mother could not get the car out. She telephoned the school and told the teacher to tell the little girl to walk home and be very careful as she walked on the ice. Anxiously the mother waited. At last she saw the little girl coming up the sidewalk with one hand raised as if holding on to someone's hand, but there was no one with her. At the steps, she turned, bowed and smiled and opened the door. The mother asked her why she had been holding her hand up in the air. She said; God was holding her hand.

A Sunday Morning Hold-Up

"Will a man rob God? Yet ye have robbed me. In tithes and offerings." Malachi 3:8

"Upon the first day of the week, let every one of you lay by him in store as God hath prospered him, that there be no gatherings when I come." 1 Corinthians 16:2

We are living in a society which is characterized by wholesale crime. Crimes of every description are being committed every hour in the day and every minute in the hour. Our law enforcement agencies are overworked; our courts are overloaded and our prisons are overcrowded because of our crime-ridden society.

There was a time when we thought of crime as a problem which existed primarily in the ghettos and slums of our large cities. Most of us have made references to the inner-city jungle and the many dangers which exist therein. But in recent years, crime has infiltrated the suburbs so that our outlying areas and our affluent, exclusive neighborhoods offer no more safety than the black alleys in the downtown section of the city.

And then in recent weeks, our nation has seen a rash of bank robberies. In New York City as well as other metropolitan areas, banks are being robbed with increasing frequency. People who are either too lazy, too proud or too "lowdown" to work, want to enjoy the same comforts and luxuries afforded by those who earn their living by engaging in some form of profitable labor. Therefore, to satisfy their greed, they commit armed robberies, burglaries and crimes of every description.

Now, most of us who like to think of ourselves as law-abiding citizens and especially those who look upon ourselves as members of the Christian community abhor and utterly detest this devastating crime-wave which is puncturing the very fabric and fiber of our society.

We look upon bank robbers, burglars, thieves, safe-crackers, pickpockets and purse-snatchers as being untouchables; the scum of the human race and we consider them to be unfit to live in a civilized society and to dwell among decent people.

We think of their conduct base being low, despicable and inexcusable. Yet, my friends, many of those same people who would never think of shoplifting, burglarizing a house or holding up a supermarket, pull a robbery at the church every Sunday morning. Give me your undivided attention and think about something very seriously.

What would be your reaction if when you left this building and walked down the front steps, a policeman would be waiting and he would inform you that you were under arrest? How would you respond if when you asked him with what crime you were charged, he would tell you that you were charged with robbing God? How would you feel if he then read you your rights, handcuffed you, put you in the police car, took you down to the city hall and booked you? How would you react to something like that?

Now all of this might seem strange, far-fetched and out of the ordinary, but it would happen to the great majority of churchgoers if God enforced his laws in the same manner which the government enforces its laws. Whether you realize it or not, more crimes are committed on Sunday than on any other day of the week. On that very day when many people put on their best garments and go to God's house supposedly to worship Him, they usually participate in a Sunday morning hold up.

I'm sure you're asking, "How can this be? How can we rob God?"

If that is what you're asking, your question is precisely the same as that of the Israelites during the days of the prophet Malachi.

God, speaking through his Prophet, asked this question of the children of Israel, "Will a man rob God?"

And the very thought of such a crime was so unthinkable that He answered His own question and said, "Surely not."

But then as God looked at the evidence as He allowed one of His eyes to look at the payroll book down at the plant where most of the parishioners were employed, and as He allowed His other eye to look at the amount which had been put in the collection plate.

As He allowed His x-ray eyes to look on the inside of the envelopes which the ushers had collected and as He allowed these same x-ray eyes to penetrate their leather billfolds, beautiful handbags and costly shoulder bags, and as He made a comparison of what they had given with what they had left, He said, "I've been robbed."

Well, the people wanted to know, "Who robbed You? Where and when did the robbery take place? What method was used to get your money, Lord? What weapons were used in the stick up? How many persons participated in the hold up? Who drove the getaway vehicle?"

I hear God answering, and He says in essence, "You robbed me—you who are seated in the congregation—you who call yourselves by My name. You who have been sending up petitions to the throne of grace, and you who have been listening to the preaching of the gospel. Yes, you are the robbers.

"Now, as far as the time and place are concerned, I want to tell you that the robbery took place at My house; this sacred spot where you are seated right now and the time was just a few minutes ago when the collection plates were passed. You didn't use any weapons, no guns or knives were flashed and no threats were made. It was a well-planned robbery—done so skillfully and with such precision that no one ever suspected a robbery was taking place.

"As a matter of fact, at the very time some of you were robbing Me, you were singing "You can't beat God giving." And then to top it all off, when you finished robbing Me, you had someone to stand up and ask My blessing upon the robbery. You further asked Me to bless those who robbed Me and also to bless those who were not able to rob me.

"Now this is the way you pulled it off. You held back a large portion of that which you owed Me. You robbed Me in tithes and offerings. Many of you are just tipping Me instead of paying your bill. I only ask you to pay Me ten percent of your income and most of you don't want to do that. Some of you pay Me five percent, two percent, one percent and some no percent.

"Only a few of you have paid your bills. I send all of you 168 hours of air to breathe every week. I send you 84 hours of sunshine and an ample supply of rain. I've been waking you up every morning since you have been alive, and not only have I been waking you up, I've been starting you out on your way. And I've been giving you enough energy, health and strength to make it through the day.

"I've put shelter over your head. I've put food on your table. I've put clothes on your back. I've put shoes on your feet. I've given you eyes to see, ears to hear, a nose to smell, a heart to love, a tongue to talk and feet to walk. I tuck you in every night and rock you to sleep and while you are slumbering, I send angelic bodyguards to stand by your bedside. And I've heard some of you singing "all night, all day, the angels watching over me, my Lord." But still you don't want to pay Me.

"On the first day of the week, instead of paying your tithes and giving your offering, you pull your weekly robbery.

"And you are so slick with your robbery that there is no need for a getaway vehicle. Before you leave the building, you stand and shake hands with your fellow robbers. You ask me to bless the tie that binds your hearts in Christian love. You ask Me to be with you until you meet for the next robbery and you march out singing "Hallelujah and Thank you Jesus." And when you get outside, there is no need to be in a hurry, because no one has the slightest idea that a robbery has just taken place.

"So, will a man rob God? Yes, it is being done every Sunday morning at My house by those who call themselves My people."

This was God's indictment against Israel, and it is His indictment against us today. By and large, we are still pulling weekly robberies.

Let's look at some of the common excuses which are given by people who do not tithe:

(Excuse) - Tithing is taught only in the Old Testament.

(Answer) - This is absolutely wrong. The word "tithe" appears 22 times in the Old Testament. In Matthew 23:23, Jesus endorses the practice of tithing by referring to the hypocrisy of the Pharisees, "Yes, you should tithe, but you shouldn't leave the more important things undone." (The Living Bible) In 1st Corinthians Paul says, *"On every Lord's Day each of you should put aside something from what you have earned during the week and use it for the offering."* The amount depends on how much the Lord has helped you to earn. While the tithe is not specified there, it is inferred. Proportionate giving has as its foundation the percentage of ten percent.

(Excuse) - "I don't make enough money to tithe."

(Answer) - God's plan is fair to everyone. These who have a small income are only required to pay a small amount. The practice of tithing is not achieved by the size of a person's income. It is achieved by the size of a person's heart.

Those persons who won't pay God one dollar out of ten, won't pay Him ten dollars out of a hundred.

(Excuse) - "I made too much money to tithe."

(Answer) - If God has blessed you to make such a large sum, how can you afford not to pay Him His share? After all, it is God who gives you the energy, strength and the know-how to earn an income. Isn't it only right that you should pay Him so that His work can be refinanced? The late John D. Rockefeller was a tither and I'm sure that none of us can boast of a fortune larger than his.

In referring to his stewardship, Rockefeller once said, "I never would have been able to tithe the first million dollars I ever made if I had not tithed my first salary which was $1.50 a week."

Now, let's look at some of the consequences of robbing God.

First, when a person takes what God has reserved for Himself and uses it for his personal wants and needs, he forfeits his claim to that amount which God has allotted for him. The tithe is a contract or a gentlemen's agreement between God and His children. Whereby God promises His blessings to those who pay Him ten percent. When we violate our end of the bargain, we have no right to expect God to honor His end of the contract.

The expulsion of Adam and Eve from the Garden of Eden is a prime example of what happens when people take what belongs to God.

Secondly, those who rob God lose their right to have any vocal input into God's program. People whose stewardship is delinquent do not have the right to manage and disburse the payments of those whose stewardship is up to par. Ironically, most of the hell in the church is raised by people who rob God every week. This is a blatant act of disrespect for God and His laws. When a person's account is delinquent, he should be found bowing at the altar begging for mercy rather than raising a fuss and keeping up confusion.

Finally, a person who robs God ultimately robs himself. God promised to open the windows of Heaven and pour out an abundant blessing upon those who followed His plan. It goes without saying it that this blessing is denied those who refuse His plan. Therefore, when we fail to tithe, we shut the windows of Heaven and prevent God from giving us what He already has in store.

It should be noted that, in reality, is it not a question of whether or not we will tithe, but to whom we will pay our tithe. God has a way of taking His ten percent out of our income. When we refuse to pay it to Him, he sometimes fixes it so that we have to pay it to someone else, a penalty is usually attached. Some people pay their tithe to the doctor, others pay it to the lawyers, some pay it to the drugstore, and others pay it to the mechanic. There are no two ways about it, God will not let us keep His money. Those who rob Him will always get caught. God's x-ray eyes are like hidden cameras and they are making pictures of every robbery we commit.

But I'm glad that He promised an abundant blessing for those who will obey His plan. God says, "Try me...prove me...put your trust in me...put me to the test...pay your bills to Me and see won't I bless you...let me show you how you can do more with 90 cents with My blessings than you can do with $1.00 without My blessing.

When My Mission Work Is Done

"Teaching them to observe all things whatsoever I have commanded you; and lo, I am with you always, even unto the end of the world. Amen" Matthew 28:20

The evangelism call is a command of God, to the church as found in Matthew 38:19-20. The word mission is an organized effort to spread mission, it is the work of a missionary and to conduct a religious mission among the people. Missionary is a person sent on a religious mission, to convert people to Christianity. That's what the preacher John is all about. He is on a mission for God. Jesus said teach them to observe all things (like how to be saved).

John said, *"But as many as received him, to them gave Him power to become the sons of God, He that believeth on me hath everlasting life."* John 5:24

Paul said, *"For I am not ashamed of the Gospel of Christ: for it is the power of God unto salvation to everyone that believeth."* Romans 1:16

But when my mission work is done I can hear the voice of the Master in the skies saying "well done, thou good and faithful servant. Thou hast been faithful over a few things, I will make thee ruler over many things." Before Moses' mission work was done, he climbed the rocky steps of Mount Sinai's lofty heights and watched the finger of God write the law of man's conduct in a slab of stone.

Before Daniel's mission work was done, he spent the night in the lion's den. Before Elijah's mission work was done, he built an altar on Mount Carmel and drenched it with water and God touched the divine switch in heaven and set the air on fire while Elijah was praying.

Don't Ever Say You Don't Like the Mission Work

Jesus called men to mission work. He first called Peter and Andrew and He called James and John, the sons of Zebedee. The words are found in Matthew 4:18-22. Now let us look at the scene where He found His missionaries. The scene was a body of water 13 miles long and 6 miles wide and was abounded with fish. This body of water had 3 names:

1. The sea or lake of Gennesaret, for at its northwestern angle was a fertile plain called Gennesaret.

2. The sea of Tiberias, for Tiberias stood with eight other cities on the shore of the sea.

3. The Sea of Galilee from the province of Galilee which bordered on the western side.

Here Jesus found the material out of which He would make Apostles but by profession they were fishermen, suppliers of the market of Galilee. By economy they were poor men. By education they were unlearned and ignorant men. By possession they only owned fishing boats and fishing tackles. But by the grace of God they were saved men. Yet, Peter was a cursing fisherman by trade. He was a Galilean. The Galileans were quick in tempter. They were easily arounds.

Andrew, Peter, James and John with their violence of temper, the people in the town of Galilee called them the sons of thunder. This looks like poor material to make missionaries but let us look at the Maker. He is of age. Yea before the hills in order stood, or the earth received its frame from endless age to endless age thou art the same.

Before fire ever fell on Mount Carmel, He was here. Before Sinai ever rocked and quaked from the foot of God, He was here. Before Enoch walked with God or before Noah received his orders to build the Ark of Mount Ararat, He was here. He is of age. Before Moses at the back side of the desert at the foot of Mount Horeb ever heard God called him from a burning bush, He was here. Before Abraham ever left the land of Ur in route to Canaan or Jacob wrestled with the angel, He was here! That being said my brothers and sisters, I got some good news. He's here right now.

God can fix you up for mission work. He has had experience creating worlds, scooping out seas with His hand, weighing mountains in scales, hills in balances, setting the planets in their orbits, sprinkling stars through his fingers and painting the sky blue without a step ladder. He has made lions lay down around the prophet Daniel and pulled Jeremiah from a murky dungeon with rotten rags. So, He is the maker of mission workers.

What did God make out of Andrew, Peter, James and

John? Andrew's missionary work began at home. He brought the lad to Jesus with his five loaves and two fishes. James was the first of the twelve to die for the word of God. John, He made him an Apostle of Love. For he wrote the love letter that said God so loved the world! Cursing Peter was made a Jerusalem Pentecostal Preacher. He was made the speaker of the apostolic house. One day, he opened doors of the church and took in 3000 members.

So God Is Able To Make A Mission Worker Out Of You!

Christ and the Common Man

"...and the common people heard him boldly..." Mark 12:37

There is sense in which it can be said that Christ was a commoner. He was born, bred and buried a common man. He did not belong to what man called the fellowship of big folk. He loved everybody but He lived among little people. He was more simple than sophisticated. Socially, politically and economically, He was identified with common people. He had a message for aristocrats but ordinary people heard it first.

His mother, Mary, was a common woman. When she discovered that He was to be her son and the world's Savior, a song was born: "My soul," she sang, "doth magnify the Lord." The sixth century Christians named her song, THE MAGNIFICANT. She says in essence in this song that of His handmaiden, He hath exalted them of low degree.

His contemporaries saw Him as a common man. The Nazarenes, who were citizens of His hometown saw Him in this manner. When in their temple He stood and read, they were made to remark, "Is not this Joseph's son?" The community of Capernaum, likewise, saw Him as a common man. When in their hearing He proclaimed Himself to be the bread of life, they murmured, "Is not this Jesus the son of Joseph whose father and mother we know?" To the Jews of Galilee, He was but average and ordinary.

When in their temple they heard Him teach, they were made to marvel, "How is it, "they said, "that this untrained man has such learning?"

Herein is another sense in which it can be said that Jesus is the son of man, for the masses of men on this earth are common people.

It is deep within my conviction that Christ's arrival as a common man was no accident. For from being a change affair, I deem it a divine arrangement. To be a divine arrangement. To be sure God could have made His final and fullest revelation in the person of prince or the son of a king. The fact in focus, however, is that He didn't. He looks, as it were, over a stratified society and selects the common type in which to become incarnate. This, to me, is studded with enduring significance.

It signifies, to begin with, that the weight of Christ's movement is opposed to the oppression which has operated against common people. This oppression is hoary with age and worn with time. In the perspective of history the masses and minorities have known misery, while the classes lived in comfort. By and large the common folk have been people of sorrow and acquainted with grief. This oppression has taken on many and varied forms. One such form is colonialism. In this system one people seek to control the destiny and confiscate the resources of another people. Most recently Africa and India have made bold strides in detaching themselves from the chariot wheels of this ism. Slavery is still another form. Your forefathers and mind were most familiar with this system.

Howard Thurman reports that as a boy it was his practice to listen to the reading of the Bible by his mother. He was careful to note that she never read anything from the Epistles of Paul. After growing up his curiosity sent him asking his mother why. She explained that the slave owners frequently sent white preachers to deliver a message to slave congregations. In most cases they would take as a test the words of Paul which were written to the Ephesians, "servants be obedient to them that are your masters." Though an uneducated slave she found it difficult to believe as Paul seemed to have made it sound, that Christ and His armies marched on the side of slavery.

SEGREGATION and second class citizenship with which we are all too well acquainted is another form used by the common man's oppressor. Godless capitalism is another form of social oppression. In this ism a few men in feudalistic pattern become the possessors of life's acknowledged goods, pays the piper and calls the tune. It is these men that James has in mind when he writes, *"Go to now, ye rich men, weep and howl for your miseries that shall come upon you. Behold the hire of the laborers who have reaped down your fields, which is of you kept back by fraud, cruet; and the cries of them which have reaped have entered into the ears of the Lord of Sabbath."*

TIME and again when this oppression has become unbearable God raised up a Moses. He sent unto our situations a Martin Luther King and tolerated the triumph of a communist movement. I am no communist nor a communist sympathizer. I am frank to admit, however, that in the communist movement the condition of the common man is brought to the foreground of history.

SECONDLY, that Christ was born a common man, signifies that common people have the capacities to rise to places of distinction and incomparable achievement. Christ scores to us that a man can move progressively from commoner to king, from the backwoods to the broad lights, from circumference to center, from peasantry to prince, from a nameless nobody to the man everybody knows and from a manger in Bethlehem to the ownership of many mansions.

I am deeply impressed with the way Stuart and Clark write the biography of Jesus. "Here is a man," they say, "who was born in and obscure village, the child of a peasant woman. He was reared up in another village, a despised one at that. He worked in a carpenter shop until the age of thirty and then became an itinerant preacher for three years. He never wrote a book. He never held an office. He never had a family. He never owned a home. He never set foot in a really big city. He never traveled, except in infancy, more than two-hundred miles from where He was born.

"WHILE still a young man the tide of public opinion turned against Him. His friends ran out. One of them betrayed Him. He was turned over to His enemies. They carried through the mockery of a trial. They nailed Him upon a cross between two thieves. While He died His executioners gambled for the only piece of property He had on earth. They took Him down from the cross and through the courtesy of a friend laid Him in a borrowed grave. Nineteen wide centuries have come and gone and yet this man is the centerpiece of history and the only real leader in human progress. I am for within the man when I say that all the armies that ever marched, all the navies that ever sailed, all the kings that ever ruled and all the parliaments that ever sat have not affected mankind like this one solitary life." (Attributed to Dr. James Allen Francis)

FINALLY, Christ as a commoner, signifies that common people could find the quest of their lives by simply casting their lot with Him. He says in effect to the common man, *"Come thou with me and I will do thee good."* To that concourse of common people who tracked His trail in Palestine He extended a great invitation and it stands to this day; *"Come unto me all you that labor and are heavy laden and I will give you rest. Take my yoke upon you and learn of me, for my yoke is easy and my burdens are light."*

It is safe to say that the common man's quest is the same basically as other people. And what is it that all people want? Well, we all want a feeling of significance. We want to count and be of consequence. We want to be crucial to something, important to someone and needed by somebody. Nothing is more of nuisance than to feel that we are unnecessary. It seems as if our oppressors have contrived conditions and calculated their moves so as to make us feel unimportant, thus hopeless, helpless and hemmed in. They've huddled us off into the nooks and corners of society. They've run governments without our voice and our vote. They've murdered us in wholesale fashion. The common people have time and again counted their dead in numbers of thousands, yea, in numbers of millions.

BECAUSE the common people are frequently without a basic self-esteem and riddled with feelings of inferiority, they do strand and silly things. They scratch where nothing itches, disdain to look their supposed superiors in the eye, duck and dodge them as often as possible and allow themselves to be caught by the hellhounds of fear, hatred and deception.

TO reduce this sense of insignificance, moreover, to rub out this feeling of inferiority, Jesus pricks and strings our consciences with a network of observations. He observes first of all that our heavenly Father needs us.

"The Harvest," he says, "truly is great but the laborers are few." He observed further that the common man is the object of God's care: "Behold the fowls of the air, for they sow not, neither do they reap, nor gather into barns; yet your heavenly Father feuded them. Are ye not much better than they?" He observes also that every man has inherent value: "Are not two sparrows sold for a farthing? And one of them shall not fall on the ground without your Father. But the very hairs of your head are all numbered. Fear ye not therefore, ye are of more value than many sparrows." With these convictions hanging on to one's conscience he can walk the streets of society with the confidence that "I'm Somebody."

FINALLY, the common people are constantly engaged in a struggle for survival. Sundry means and diverse methods are used by the common man for survival. Some seek to survive by imitating the oppressor. We are aware of how strong the urge is to destroy what is different. This is vividly portrayed in the relationship between whites and Negroes in America. More than a few Negroes believe that to be like the whites is to be exactly right. Consequently, they endeavor to dress, to have church, to have a scale of value and the like just like white people.

THERE are others who seek to survive by violence, political participation, education, economic acquisitions, and traitorship. There is, to be sure, some practical value in all of these. Notwithstanding, the key to survival according to Jesus is to join Him.

The Mailman's Mission

"Preach the word; be instant in season, out of season; reprove, rebuke, exhort with all longsuffering and doctrine." 2 Timothy 4:2

Have you ever known a mail carrier? For many years the Black community considered the job of mail carrier a prestigious position. It was hard to get, paid well and provided good benefits. The first Blacks who became mail carriers were a source of price for their neighbors and friends.

However well the job pays, being a mail carrier is a bit dangerous. There are vicious animals to consider such as dogs and other strange pets of their neighborhood. Weather conditions often make the mailman's job even harder. The post office motto: "Through wind, rain and snow, the mail must go" reads well but people really expect mail delivery, despite the weather. If it's not dogs or the weather, then it is often the residents on the route that give the mail carrier his biggest headache. He is the bearer of good news and bad news. He is hugged and kissed when he brings good news and monthly checks. He is cursed and kicked when he delivers bad news, or the checks don't come.

The postal service has thousands of mail carriers who

carry the mail in the backwoods on wagons, in swamps on boats and in Alaska on dog sleds. Whenever there are people, there is a mail carrier to serve them.

Did you know that God is a mailman? God is heaven's postmaster general and he has millions of mail carriers all over the world. These mail carriers are the ministers of the Gospel who, like the mail carrier has the job of delivering a message from heaven. As Christians, let's keep watch out for a message from heaven. Let us continue to praise the feet of them who bring us a word from the Lord, for this is truly a great work.

You see, every child of God ought to have some inside information. Every now and then, Jesus would take the disciples up into the mountain, or some desolate place and give them some inside information. God's people have been given some inside information. Because you just have to have it.

You know Satan attacked Jesus and he's not going to pass you and me up. You have to be like Jesus to be saved-you can't just act like Jesus and be saved. But Satan will tell you that you can just act like Jesus and you can be saved. He knows how to attack, if he can't get the messenger, he'll just attack the message. If he can't get the servant, he'll attack the Service. He wants us to accept the temporary and miss the eternal. You see, everything Satan has is just TEMPORARY and only what you do for CHRIST will last.

Satan doesn't use the word "KINGDOM," he puts an "S" on his kingdom, making it plural and the plurality means that there's something wrong with it. God has said, "The kingdoms of this world have become the Kingdom of our Lord and of His Christ and He shall reign forever."

Satan wants to keep our minds little, he knows that if we can see HIGH things, we can reject LOW things. So, you have to watch Satan and stay away from his parking meters. It'll cost you when you park in his zone-he fines us, locks us up, gives us tickets and in so many ways, some of our fines are to be flat on our backs, in a hospital, with some malignant disease, car wrecks, separations, divorces. Our kids going to the penitentiary, overdoses of dope, sittin' up all night worrying about a child that didn't come in. We pay in so many ways. So, it is better for God's people to keep on moving and not try to park here-this world is not our home. Jesus went to Calvary and died to point us in the direction of heaven. That lets us know that we're not to park here.

We must keep on moving, in spite of our sicknesses, we can't park. In spite of our troubles, we can't park here. In spite of the miseries, this world is not our parking place.

In our text, the children of Israel have been in bondage for 430 years and God has sent Moses and Aaron to tell Pharaoh to "Let my people go."

Moses led them out of bondage, out through the desert, out from under the whip and they've come face to face with the Red Sea. There were mountains on each side and Pharaoh's Army behind-and now they wanted to park right there.

They began to cry, "WHY BRING US OUT HERE TO

DIE? WE WOULD HAVE BEEN BETTER OFF IF WE HAD STAYED IN EGYPT, at least we had some food and water and a graveyards. Now, Moses has brought us here to die."

But it's a mighty bad thing to park in this world. God told Moses to stretch out his Rod and the Red Sea opened up and the crossed on dry land. They were so happy that they organized a choir on their way across and as soon as they reached the other side, they wanted to park right there. Then they started grumbling against God.

They told Moses to tell God, "Come and talk to us. Let Him tell us what He wants us to know."

Then God told Moses to get back out of the way and thunder began to roar, lightening began to flash and the whole world began to reel and rock.

They said to Moses, "Moses, tell God to hush. We'll listen to you, God talked too loud."

I'm so glad, this morning, that this world is not my home.

I'm just a pilgrim and a stranger traveling through this barren land.

THEN, I HEARD JESUS SAY;

"I can't park in the garden."

"I can't park on the cross."

"I can't park in the grave."

"I can't park in the Upper Room."

And He stepped on a cloud and rode back to glory.

Little Preachers and Big People

"And the Lord sent Nathan unto David. And David's anger was greatly kindled against the men and he said to Nathan as the Lord liveth the man that hath done this thing shall surely die. And Nathan said to David; thou art the man." 11 Samuel 12:1, 5, 7

When a man gets big and important he usually feels that he is independent and self-sufficient within himself and very often he does not really feel that he is particularly subject to anyone, not even God. This attitude often leads him to falsely assume that he himself is the criteria for all things and especially where his conduct and desire are concerned.

True it is that most big people were once little but too often many of them forget the GOD who stood by them and made them big.

Our Message today brings us to the palaver of King, A great and powerful King. A King whose life and accomplishments speak of a super somebody whose wisdom and power had lifted him from the lowly humble level of a country shepherd boy to a realm of riches and the reign of a Glorious Kingdom. Here was a King who was a Master of Music, a potentate of Poetry, A Super-Soldier, A Legendary Leader, one wise in

Wisdom, Pragmatic in Philosophy, deeply devoted, reverently religious and full of the satisfaction of a life well-lived and a goal well gained.

At heart he was inclined toward good and GOD, but in actuality he was sort of stuck on himself. And well he might be for he had merited the esteem of both man and God. He had won his way amid the trials and besetments of life. He had proven himself to be a prince even as a pauper. He had lifted himself, as it were by his very bootstraps. He had won both fame and fortune in his noble conquest over his enemies and now he had found his place in a Palace.

He was a Big Man on the other hand, Nathan as just a humble little Preacher. But this Preacher as it true with all of God's Preachers, had a part to play in the providence of God.

He was just a little Preacher, but all Preachers have a purpose.

1. It is the purpose of the Preacher to help us see ourselves as we really are.

2. It is the purpose of the Preacher not to condemn nor condone. But to help us measure ourselves by the approval of a good conscience.

3. It is the purpose of the Preacher to help us examine our own character and conduct by the same standards that we require of others.

4. It is the purpose of the Preacher to proclaim the true nature of God. To take heed to his wisdom and the goodness and mercy. TO Tell of his Patience and loving kindness, his justice and judgment.

5. It is the purpose of the Preacher to preach the eternal work of God and the immutable of it, for God cannot lie and he does not lie.

6. It is the purpose of the preacher to tell us how good the LORD has been to us.

The Preachers are God's Prophets. They are the proclaimers of the good news of the gospel of GOD. They are to sound the note of repentance. They are the voice of one crying in the wilderness.

DAVID HAD COMMITTED a Grieving sin in ordering Urias to the head of the battle to be killed. The real reason for this action was his desire to have Urias' wife as his own.

GOD sent his Preacher to the place of King David to warn him of his sin.

Many times the Preacher is called upon in the performance of his duties to bring indictment to those who have run counter to the laws of God. It is not the Preacher's job to condemn. His job is but to speak the words as GOD commands.

Hot Lips and Cold Heart

"Wherefore the Lord said; forasmuch as the people draw near me with their mouth and with their lips do honor me, but have removed their hearts far from me and their fear toward me is taught by precept of men." Isaiah 29:13

Webster's definition of the word lip, and I quote, is "the two fleshy folds forming the edge of the mouth." Anyone that knows anything know this, something we learn without going to school, you don't have to go to school to know where your mouth is. You don't have to go to school to learn what to do with your mouth. Automatically we know we speak through it, this is one of the few things we learn early in life, where the mouth is and how to use it.

The Lord is speaking to his people through the prophet, Isaiah concerning lip service and there is a whole lot of that going on in the world today. If folks could talk their way to Heaven nobody would to go hell. Just to listen to some folks talk, you would say to yourself that individual is going to heaven whole soul and body. He is going like Elijah went. But you just follow him around the corner, that same person who had so much religion in his lips don't have any in his heart. So many folks talk Christianity and do just the opposite.

Some folks say they love you and won't speak to you.

So many folks have lots of lip and nothing to back it up with. Talk is cheap, if you want to buy land you have to have some money. Look if you will, at the characters of this man of God, Isaiah. Several things are known of him.

First, he was called to his work the last year of the reign of Uzziah. Secondly, he lived at Jerusalem during the reign of Uzziah, Jokam, Ahaz and Hezekiah. Most of his life seems to have been spent in the courts around Uzziah. God had to move Uzziah so he could use him to tell the people what he wanted them to know. As long as Uzziah was living, seemingly Isaiah couldn't see the Lord. So Isaiah said it was in the year that King Uzziah died I saw the Lord. He is the most renowned of all the Old Testaments Prophets. He spoke for all nations and for all times. He was a man of powerful intellect, great integrity and remarkable force of character. He is quoted in the New Testament more than any of the other prophets.

Because of the relationship of his teaching to the New Testament times, they have been called the bridge between the old and new covenant. He was married, had two sons, and this man brings a message from God to his people.

Two important factors which will mean much in the judgment. For with lips we speak, with hearts we believe. The Lord Jesus said, "If you are ashamed to own me before men, I will be ashamed to own you before my father." So we can see that lips are very important in this Christian journey.

Some folks profess to know Jesus and seemingly they

are ashamed to own Him. If you are ashamed to own Him here, when you face Him in the Judgment, He is going to be ashamed to tell the Father, "This is one of my jewels."

The tenth chapter of Paul's letter to the Roman Church says in part, "If thou shalt confess with thy mouth and believe in thy heart that God hath raised him from the dead, thou shalt be saved."

So, we can see in this that lips are very essential to salvation. Look again at "Hot Lips" if you will, David said; *"They speak vanity, everyone against his neighbor, with flattering lips and with a double heart do they speak."*

We find this in everyday life, people saying one thing with their lips and meaning another in their heart. Some folks know they don't mean what they say, but they say it anyway. This is what I am saying—just to hear some folks pray you'll think that his heart is on hallowed fire, and there is nothing burning but his lips.

Some folks have hot lips but they are lying lips, and that is bad. Those are the hottest kind of lips. They are so hot they will get you killed. They will make folks hate you without a cause. Lying lips are dangerous lips. I would rather face a rattlesnake or a hungry lion than to face lying lips. Maybe I would have a chance to get away from a lion or rattler, but it just takes so long to outgrow lying lips.

Some folks are just prone to lying. Some folks lie so much until they believe it themselves. A fellow lied so much until he told everybody that there was going to be a ball game this evening.

When everybody got there and the players never showed up he said, "Man, you know I forgot I was lying."

He believed it himself.

Well let me tell you what David said here about lying lips. *"Let lying lips be put to silence which speaketh grievous things, proudly and contemptuously against the righteous."* Some folks enjoy lying on the righteous. They enjoy lying on Jesus. Listen! When Jesus was sitting with publicans and sinners, they went and told everybody. "This man who says he is the Son of God is nothing but a wine bibber." They saw him on Sunday, got hungry—you need to eat on Sunday as well as you do on Monday—went down in the cornfield and pulled some corn so they could eat. They told folks, "This man who says he is God's Son is nothing but a law breaker," lying on him. You don't stop eating because today is Sunday. We are talking about hot lips and cold hearts.

You see "hot lips with a cold heart" don't mean a thing as far as God is concerned. Your lips can be so hot you can see fire coming off of them, but if your heart is cold, you are in a bad fix.

Hot lips are deceiving. They conceal a cold heart. Everybody you see laughing at you don't mean it. Folks can laugh with you, and their heart is like a deep freeze.

But I am glad today God can look through those blazing lips and see that frigid heart. Look again if you will how hot lips set with a cold heart. You shake hands with someone and barely have hold of two fingers. That's a cold heart behind that hand shake. Shake hands with you smiling, and when they smile you see wrinkles under their eyes. That's a gold heart—a gold heart will wrinkle up your eyes. When you smile with a warm heart, your eyes light up. There is a glow in your eyes.

The Japanese Ambassador had hot lips and a cold heart. He was talking peace in Washington in 1941 and bombing Pearl Harbor. That's what hot lips and a cold heart will do. Folks talking good to you and digging dirt from under your feet, talking sweet to you and digging a ditch for you on the other end. Hot lips and a cold heart, according to the allegations I heard from Richard Millhouse Nixon, had hot lips and a cold heart. He was talking to the American public and concealing Watergate. He had hot lips and a cold heart.

What Did You Come to Church For?

Scriptural Background John 5:9b-15
(KJV) *Afterward Jesus findeth him in the temple and said unto him, "Behold, thou art made whole: sin no more, lest a worse thing come unto thee." (14)*
(TJB) *After a while Jesus met him in the Temple and said, "Now you are well again, be sure not to sin any more, or something worse may happen to you." (14)*
(NIV) *Later Jesus found him at the temple and said to him, "See, you are well again. Stop sinning or something worse may happen to you." (14)*

The early church (apostolic) began as a place for prayer, praise and edification. Today I want to talk about praise, prayer and edification in response to the work of the Holy Spirit. We hope to answer two questions: What is a person supposed to do AFTER being blessed by the Holy Spirit? What good reason would anyone have to come to church?

You recognize this event takes place just after the 38-year-old man had been healed by Jesus. It is evident that he was A RELIGIOUS PERSON.

- He had frequented a place where he hoped for what he believed to be a religious experience in healing, i.e. getting into the water AFTER it was stirred by an angel.

- He went straightway (it was Sabbath) to the Temple afterward.

- He was grateful for what had taken place, so it was "natural" for him to go to church to give thanks (praise). (NOTE: The Greek ainoe>ainos means "praise returned for benefits received or expected, Zhodiates.")

If a believer has received benefits from God, he or she should come to the House of God and PRAISE Him.

One of the things a person should come to the church (temple) for assuredly is to PRAISE GOD!

1 Peter 5:8 warns us to *"Be sober, be vigilant; because your adversary the devil, as a roaring lion, walketh about, seeking whom he may devour."*

It is only a matter of time before we will be staring in the face of today's faith adversaries. It may be Goliath, the giant of a troubled home; or Goliath, the giant of a prolonged illness. We must be willing to face our difficulties, relying on our God-given strength.

DAVID RESPONDED TO THE CHALLENGE OF GOLIATH BY ANSWERING, "FOR WHO IS THIS UNCIRCUMCISED PHILISTINE, THAT HE SHOULD DEFY THE ARMIES OF THE LIVING GOD."

He answered this challenge with his faith in a "God that would deliver him." It was not his physical stature or fighting ability that caused him to stand up to Goliath, but his trust in God. He told the Philistine, *"Thou comest to me with a sword and with a spear and with a shield but I come to thee in the name of the LORD of hosts, the God of the armies of Israel, whom thou hast defied."* 1 Samuel 17:45

AFTER DEFEATING GOLIATH, THE PHILISTINE, DAVID HAD TO CONFRONT THE CHALLENGE OF A JEALOUS KING SAUL.

Sometimes those whom we have trusted in the past can become our new enemies. Oftentimes, Satan is defeated in our alien enemies, only to reappear in the jealousy of our brothers or sisters. We must stand our ground in faith and answer this challenge by not becoming bitter and retaliatory; but "...love your enemies, bless them that curse you, do good to them that hate you and pray for them which despitefully use you and persecute you." (Matthew 5:44) Saints never go about trying to *get even*.

"For the weapons of our warfare are not carnal but mighty through God to the pulling down of strongholds." (2 Corinthians 10:4)

THE REAL SERVANT OF GOD NOT ONLY ANSWERS THE THREATS FROM HIS ADVERSARIES BUT ALSO ANSWERS THE CHALLENGES OF DISCIPLESHIP AND EVANGELISM.

Jesus said that in Matthew 24:14. *"This gospel of the kingdom shall be preached in all the world for a witness unto all nations and then shall the end come."*

Christians will answer the challenge of financing the work of our Lord on the earth. Dedicated believers will always make sure the resources are available to do ministry for Christ. They will have a "liberal heart" to give to the poor realizing that *"he that hath pity upon the poor lendeth unto the Lord and that which he hath given will he pay him again."* (Proverbs 19:17)

THE WORD OF GOD BEGAN IN MANY OF HIS SERVANTS-NOT BY THEIR AMBITION BUT BY THEIR ANSWER TO A CHALLENGE.

Isaiah became the messianic prophet by answering the challenge of becoming a spokesman for God in Israel. In his testimony in Isaiah 6:8 he relates, "I heard the voice of the Lord saying, *'Whom shall I send and who will go for us? Then said I, Here am I; send me.'"*

Isaiah answered this great challenge and gave us a description of our redeemer. He was able to give Israel descriptions of their approaching Savior and Messiah, *"a child is born, unto us a son is given and the government shall be upon His shoulder and His name shall be called Wonderful, Counselor, the Mighty God, the Everlasting Father, the Prince of Peace."* (Isaiah 9:6)

ISAIAH BECAME THE PROPHET WHO WAS ABLE TO PREDICT DETAILS OF THE FORM OF "CHRIST IN THE EARTH."

Isaiah 53:5-7 tells us that this redeemer would be wounded for our transgressions. *"He was bruised for our iniquities. The chastisement of our peace was upon Him and with His stripes we are healed."*

The book of Revelation tells us how Christ became our Savior as no one was found who was able to open the book (volume of instructions in righteousness) breaking bondage of sin and loosing man from the "penalty of death." Revelations 5:5 says, *"And one of the elders saith unto me, 'Weep not: behold, the Lion of the Tribe of Judah, the Root of David, hath prevailed to open the book, and to loose the seven seals thereof.'"*

Whatever the 38-year-old man was doing or not doing was causing him to MISS God. In so doing he became ILL and/or was sustaining his own illness.

What about your illnesses today? What did you do? Who do you need to forgive? What stands between you and a wholesome relationship with God?

Now the major question: WHAT DID YOU COME TO CHURCH FOR:

    I Hope you came to Pray

    I Hope you came to give PRAISE for what the Holy Spirit has done for you.

    I Hope you came to meet JESUS.

    I Hope you came to hear Him say to you: STOP SINNING!

MAYBE IF YOU STOP YOU WILL RECEIVE AN OUTPOURING OF THE HOLY SPIRIT UPON YOU and have MORE to thank and praise God for.

Answering a Challenge

SUBTOPIC: Don't sit down Stand Up...When the Devil moves in the church kick him out and let the church roll on.

"And as he talked with them behold, there came up the champion, the Philistine of Gath, Goliath by name, out of the armies of the Philistines and spake according to the same words, and David heard (them)." 1 Samuel 17:23 (KJV)

We can unexpectedly become giant-killers when we stand up to fight tremendous challenges to our discipleship. In the text we find Goliath appearing and challenging the people of Israel to battle. To utilize the immense size of their warrior, Goliath, the Philistines desired for a one-on-one contest with any Israelite.

GOLIATH WAS THEIR "BIG GUN."

His size was extraordinary to say the least. If a cubic is 21 inches, he was over 11 feet in height—if about 18 inches, he was over 9 feet. The Philistines had invaded territory, which belonged to Israel, and Goliath was sent daily to challenge any man to personal combat. 1 Samuel 17:11 reveals that Saul and the armies of Israel were dismayed and afraid of this giant. The expected defenders of Israel were powerless to "respond" to the challenge and this challenge went unanswered for 40 days until David heard the threat.

DAVID DID NOT ACTIVELY SEEK OUT GOLIATH FOR A FIGHT.

His father, Jesse, instructed him to go to the battlefield with food for his older brothers. Verse 23 reveals two very important facts. First, while talking with his brethren on the battlefield, Goliath came up to them and issued his same battle challenge. Secondly, the verse states that David's brethren ran and left him to answer the giant alone. Truly it was a matter of David's being in the "wrong place" at the "wrong time."

YOU DO NOT HAVE TO GO LOOKING FOR THE ADVERSARY OF YOUR FAITH.

One thing the man did not expect to find in the church was criticism and condemnation. It was the church people, seeing the man carrying his pallet on the Sabbath, who interrupted their act of worship to condemn the man for "working" on the Sabbath, carrying his pallet.

The church people were not only shocked to see someone carrying a mat on the Sabbath into the church, but were further shocked to see who was carrying the mat—the man they'd known for years as a crippled beggar unable to walk. They should have joined with the man and praised God to see him walking, jumping up and down, and praising the Lord. This was a man they knew and had seen many times. (The devil doesn't like to see people praising God.)

One of the things that is supposed to happen when we come to church, in addition to prayer and praise, is edification (Greek: oikodomi(e); spiritual profit or advancement; see 1 Corinthians 14:3,5). Edification was the next thing this man was to experience. However, he did not expect to run into Jesus in the "Temple." He was even happier to find out just who Jesus was (the one who said, "Pick up your mat."). Oh, he probably thanked Jesus on sight. (Prayed, maybe not even aloud.) But had he been EDIFIED? To come face to face with Jesus, to hear Him, to obey Him, to be blessed by Him is to be edified.

It is not enough to run into Jesus or have a direct encounter with him. He will take advantage of such occasions, especially for YOUR spiritual advancement. He told the man HOW to advance spiritually. (We would say, "Become a better Christian.")

"STOP SINNING," Jesus said, the only recorded instance where Jesus said this to a person with whom He had shared in their healing.

We learn something else in the Temple. There is a correlation between being an invalid or a cripple and sinning.

What is sin? The Greek word, Hamartano (Zhodiates) a sinner is "one who keeps missing the mark in his or her relationship to God." To miss, not to hit, this mark is to SIN-To let something come between God and Us.

Jesus said that in Matthew 24:14, *"This gospel of the kingdom shall be preached in all the world for a witness unto all nations and then shall the end come."* Christians will answer the challenge of financing the work of our Lord on the earth. Dedicated believers will always make sure that the resources are available to do ministry for Christ. Thy will have a "liberal heart" to give to the poor realizing that *"he that hath pity upon the poor lendeth unto the LORD and that which he hath given will he pay him again."* Proverbs 19:17

THE WORD OF GOD BEGAN IN MANY OF HIS SERVANTS—NOT BY THEIR AMBITION BUT BY THEIR ANSWER TO A CHALLENGE.

Isaiah became the messianic prophet by answering the challenge of becoming a spokesman for God in Israel. In his testimony in Isaiah 6:8 he relates, *"I heard the voice of the Lord saying, 'Whom shall I send and who will go for us?' Then I said, 'Here am I, send me.'"*

Isaiah answered this great challenge and gave us a description of our redeemer. He was able to give Israel descriptions of their approaching Savior and Messiah. *"A child is born, unto us a son is given and the government shall be upon His shoulder and His name shall be called Wonderful, Counselor, the Mighty God, the Everlasting Father, the Prince of Peace."* (Isaiah 9:6)

ISAIAH BECAME THE PROPHET WHO WAS ABLE TO PREDICT DETAILS OF THE FORM OF "CHRIST IN THE EARTH."

Isaiah 53:5-7 tells us that this redeemer would be wounded for our transgressions. He was bruised for our iniquities. The chastisement of our peace was upon him and with his stripes we are healed.

The book of Revelation tells us how Christ became our Savior as no one was found who was able to open the book (volume of instructions in righteousness). Breaking the bondage of sin and loosing man from the "penalty of death."

Prevailed to open the book and to loose the seven seals thereof, Jesus answered the call to be our perfect sacrifice for sin when God no longer had pleasure in dead sacrifices. The writer in Hebrews related Christ's challenge to become a living sacrifice *"Wherefore when he cometh unto the world, he saith, Sacrifice and offering thou wouldest not, but a body hast thou prepared me."* (Hebrew 10:5)

JESUS WAS CHALLENGED IN HIS HUMANITY TO AVOID THE SUFFERING OF CALVARY.

He answered this challenge from his "flesh" to say *"if it be possible, let this cup pass"* with an answer to His Father, "Not my will but let thine be done." He hung between Heaven and Earth and completed God's plan of salvation for lost humanity. He answered the challenge to hate by praying for those that hated him.

Breaking Down Walls

There was division in the church at Ephesus. A racial and social division ran along the lines of Jews and Gentiles.

The Jews were the upper crust, the Gentiles were the intruders. The Jews were the called, the Gentiles were the scorned and rejected. The Jews were the circumcised, the Gentiles were the uncircumcised. The Jews had been there a long time, the Gentiles had just gained entrance.

The Jews understood the importance of the Mosaic Law. On the other hand, the Gentiles were babes, just learning this new religion. As a result of the Jews' longevity and the Gentiles just entering, there was within the church community a strong sense of strife.

Although there was strife and divisions among these two groups, the temple at Jerusalem did not help to resolve those differences, for it was a temple divided. It was not simply divided spiritually, but it was divided physically. They (the builders of the temples) had divided the worshippers into classes. The Jews could only go so far, and there was a wall. Beyond that wall sat the women. Beyond that wall were the Gentiles. Every man and woman behind a wall.

Those walls created division—they created strife. The walls meant separation. They divided husbands from wives, men from women, Jews from Gentiles.

Now walls, at one time, had a place of importance. Isaiah declared, *"A watchman ought to stand on the wall to warn the city of danger."* The wall was also used to watch over the city. On the wall, the watchman had a good view of the city. The wall had become an important issue in Nehemiah's day, so much so that he sought permission of the king, while in captivity, to go home and rebuild the walls of Jerusalem and the gates.

As long as the wall is there, no one can sense the sorrow and pain you have. As long as the wall is there, no one can see the tears you've shed in the wee hours of the night. As long as there is a wall, there is a defense mechanism. I cannot see you, you cannot see me. I cannot sense you, neither can you sense me. I cannot understand you, nor you me. Therefore, it is hard to appreciate one another.

So the walls become destructive to the very purpose and priority of the church. Remember, it was these same walls that divided Jews from Gentiles, women from men in the Temple of God.

There is a danger in the church today that we will be guilty of rebuilding those walls which Jesus has already torn down.

Now there are two kinds of walls used in buildings. There is a bearing wall-designed to bear the weight of the structure. It can bear the weight of the roof but it must be connected to the foundation. To be a wall, a bearing wall, without a foundation is useless.

You and I need that kind of wall in our lives to sustain the weight of trials, problems, difficulties, tribulations that confront us daily. But if it is not connected to that Rock of Ages, it is merely just another wall.

And there is a middle wall. This wall is an interior wall. It is a wall that can be moved and the building will still stand. But the problem with interior walls is that we create them. The middle wall is the wall of prejudices, jealousy, envy, malice and misunderstanding.

The Apostle Paul, in writing to the church at Ephesus said, *"Jesus saw the walls that had divided men and women, circumcised from uncircumcised, Jews from Gentiles and He broke down that middle wall of partition."*

Have you allowed Him to break down the walls in your life? Those walls can only be broken when you acknowledge your humanity. When you realize that you are no more than anyone else, your walls will be broken. When you acknowledge that there is nothing to hide you nor secure you. Walls are funny things. They can invade our lives physically, they influence us mentally, and they bother us psychologically and spiritually.

First of all, a wall can be a defense mechanism to shut out, to protect me from you and you from me. Are you aware of this kind of wall? Does it lurk in your mind? That wall of defense defends us from being known for what we really are. If there is no wall, we can see each other's weaknesses. You can see my weakness, and I can see yours. But, with the wall, you can't see my weakness, and I can't see yours. With the wall, we can shield ourselves, protect ourselves and defend ourselves. Some people act as if they don't have any faults. Those are the ones you'd better be aware of. They are always placing that wall of defense before them. That wall needs to be torn down so that you and I can be who folk have already perceived us to be and God knows us to be.

Then there is a wall which prevents communication. This wall exists to perpetuate misunderstanding because as long as the wall is there, we know that someone is talking, we just cannot or wish not to understand what is being said. In the temple there was talking going on from the front of the temple but because of the walls, no one could clearly understand what was being said. And as long as you do not understand what others are saying, then there is no communication.

There may be someone today who has allowed this wall to block out what which was greatly needed. I've come today to tear down that wall that has caused you to not understand me. I don't mind you leaving here disagreeing with something I've said, but I don't want you to misunderstand what I said. When I preach, my prayer to God is to be understood. There is such a thing as disagreeing without being disagreeable.

A wall can also prevent sight. Those three classes of people in the temple could not see one another. The Jews could not see the women, the women could not see the Gentiles. The wall prevented them from seeing each other.

Now, if I had a big "S" on my chest, with x-ray vision, I could see through your wall, but I do not. Therefore, as long as the wall is there, no one can see the smile behind the frown and no one is able to share in your joy.

The Unique Position of the Gospel Preacher in This Disgraced Social Order

"And He said unto them, go ye into all the world and preach the Gospel to every creature." Mark 16:15

Unique: Of which there is but one, sole, only having no equal. Rare and unusual.

We are face to face with many trying problems, which problems have made philosophers, scientists and educators rush to their libraries looking for descriptive adjectives, even adding new words to the dictionary hoping to find suitable words to describe this age in which we live.

Sodom and Gomorrah is not to be compared in wickedness, nor Corinth with all of her filth and ungodliness. Nevertheless, God has not left us without a way out.

God has a Passover for every Egypt. God has a pillar of fire by night for every dark trail. God has a pillar of Cloud for every boiling sun of hot trials. God has a passing across every Jordan of every seemingly uncrossable obstacle.

This is a disgraced society: in politics, education and sad to say, but I am compelled to say, in the church. The Church that Jesus left in the hands of the minister, we have allowed boards, heads of departments, unconverted workers and over ambitious laymen to take over where God left the minister.

We are separated people: in dress, in conduct, in conversation, in loyalty, in gratitude, in firmness and in spirituality. This America that boasts of being the "land of the free and the home of the brave."

First of all, we are not free. It is dangerous to walk the street or even remain at home. I do not refer to the intimidation we meet with other races, but we are against one another.

The Church is not suffering because of the action of Birmingham, Selma, Montgomery nor Mississippi, yet that is a part of it. Think of the suffering, the wars, the head on collisions, the airplane crashes. This is a disgraced world, and sin is the cause of it all. There are those persons on board the ship who should listen to the advice of the man with the keys in his hands. Paul was prisoner on board, but he had the keys. He told the ship officers not to set sail, for the voyage would only bring danger and frustration. He knew what he was talking about, for there stood by him that night an angel of God, whose he was. Biblical records will show that God has sustained the prophets in all ages. He is God's Key Man.

Enoch walked on by the moon and speaking in a common term, he threw love kisses at the stars and played "tic-tac" with the sun. Elijah was escorted with courtesy of God sending the sun in the form of a chariot. Paul makes it very beautiful. *"We are troubled on every side yet not in distress, perplexed but not in despair, persecuted but not destroyed, for we that are in this tabernacle do groan."*

All of this approving ourselves ministers of God, in patience, afflictions, necessities, in distresses, in stripes, in imprisonment, in tumult and in labor.

By pureness, by knowledge, by longsuffering, by kindness, by the Holy Ghost, by love unfeigned. By honor and dishonor, as unknown and yet well known. As poor yet making many rich. In other words, I hold a very unique position in the set of the Kingdom of God. I can unlock and tap the resources of God. Break up prisons, call fire out of Heaven, walk on water, and fill the widow's meal barrel.

This is a disturbed social order. We have never had so many fine houses and such few homes. We have never had so many elaborate schools and yet so many dropouts. We have never had so many hospitals and yet so many with no beds available. We have never had so many deacons, and yet we run to courts with much of our church affairs. We have never had so many ushers and yet very little peace and order in the church.

Scientifically, the world is supposed to be round, radically it is one sided. Mathematically, it is divided. Domestically, it is crooked. Educationally, it is top heavy. Geometrically, it is out of reach. Biologically, it is beyond reasoning. Athletically, it is in a hurry. Musically, it is out of tune. Spiritually it is cold and flat. But you are God's Key Man and you are equal to the situation.

God's minister holds a very unique position, you are a minister, not a mystical misfit.

You are a preacher, not just a public speaker. You are chosen of God not a choice of yours. You are elected of

God, not of the crowd. Your authority is from Heaven, not Washington. You are not a fisherman by trade but must catch men. You are not a philanthropist, but you must endower and assure some fallen man of eternal life. You are not a banker, but you must give specification and plans for the construction of God's church. You are not a doctor but you must lay hands on the sick.

You are not the captain of the Salvation Army but thousands of underprivileged must be clothed by your command. You are not a pugilist but must fight the good fight. You are not an athlete but you must run this race with patience. You are not a pilot on the old ship, but you must give directions to the old ship of Zion. You are not the director of the Red Cross, but you must bind up broken hearts on the battlefield of life.

You are not a parasite, but you are dependent on God for your sustenance. You are not a Mathematician, but you will have to add to your virtue faith and to faith knowledge. You are not liked by everyone, but you must love them that hate you. You are not a rogue, but you have to steal away sometimes and pray. You are not a policeman, but your message must arrest teenage gangs on the school campus and apprehend the drunkard.

You are not an employer to hire men, but you must tell that the wages of sin is death. You are not afraid of anyone, but like a child of God, you must sometimes hide yourself. You are not a king but you must reign over the church of God with diligence. You are not a lion, but you must be harmless as a dove.

You are not representing the blood banks of Texas,

but you must point men to that fountain filled with blood drawn from Emmanuel's veins. You are not a musician, but you must have men, women, boys and girls know that they must sing unto the Lord a new song. You are not a lawyer, but there are men who are locked in prison of hate and must be told, "Whosoever the Son sets free is free indeed." You are not the President of the USA, but all papers, documents, contracts and checks should bear your signature.

As I close this little message and take my seat, I don't know about you, but one thing I know. Letters make words, and words make sentences, and sentences tell stories. Do you hear what I'm saying? Tell how Jesus died. Tell how He got up from the dead. Tell how He raised the dead and gave sight to the blind. Tell a dying world that He is an unusual God, and He died an unusual death. He died before dinner, they buried Him before supper, and before breakfast, He got up with all power.

Bring Me the Book

I shall concern myself to the topic, "The Bible or the Book." This Book that we are speaking about today, is the Bible, the Word of God. The Bible is a special revelation from God. It was written by inspired men. Men specially guided by God's Spirit so that God might use human hands to write in his book just what he wanted them to write. God used about forty men in writing the Bible, some of these writers are unknown. The time in which these writers worked included about fifteen hundred years, from the year 1400 B.C. to 100 years after Christ. The perfect harmony of these writers is convincing evidence that all of them were guided by one mind. The mind of God.

The Bible the Book We Teach

The term "Bible" according to its original derivation means the books. It is the book of books. A divine library of sixty-six books and yet just one book. There were many books in the library of Ezra, the scribe, but he was not asked to bring a book, but was told to bring the book.

The name we use for the book is the Bible, and it's from Greek origin being derived from the word, Biblos and means the Book or Books. The language of the Book was translated from the original Hebrew language into Greek and was first written on leather rolls or papyrus and was called the Scroll!

The first book of the Bible, the book of Genesis, is the first proof that the Bible is the inspired writing of men guided by the Holy Spirit. For the book of Genesis contains events, which came to a close some 300 years before Moses was born. Therefore, with Moses being the writer, it is plain that he could have gotten his information only by direct revelation from God. In the year 374 A.D. Jerome, a Greek and Latin scholar, retired to the desert and spent four years in study of the Hebrew language. In the year 379 he was ordained, a priest at Antioch, and in 382 he went to Rome, where he was in close association with the pope. There he attained great popularity and influence by his learning and his eloquence of speech.

Later Jerome went to Bethlehem, where he spent the last 34 years of his life on this earth. Now, while we have no part of the Bible in handwriting of the original author himself, we have two kinds of sources from which we can learn. These are called manuscripts and versions. Manuscripts are documents written by hand before printing was invented, and version is a translation of any documents into another language.

So when Ezra was told to bring the BOOK, he was asked to bring the ole ancient scroll, which contained the doctrine and law of God. The book, which contains the written law and doctrine revealed to man by the Holy Spirit. Listen, God is the god of established laws from which we have a body of teaching known as doctrine, and the BIBLE IS THE BOOK in which both the law and doctrine are written. Listen to me if you please—for man to be saved he must believe and repent. He must obey the law or commands of God.

Help Me. This is why the people gathered themselves together in the streets of Jerusalem and said to Ezra the priest, "BRING ME THE BOOK. Bring the BIBLE with you." The people knew that somewhere along the line, they had gone wrong. Was it because they had failed to listen, or was it that they had been misled? Only the BOOK would tell, so bring the BOOK. They did not want their Minister to stand before them saying, I heard this, or I heard that, but rather BRING us the BOOK. Whatever the problem, whether it be finance, sickness, loneliness, the answer is in the Book.

So bring me the BOOK.

Listen, the astronauts and space scientists in checking the position of the sun, moon and other planets out in space — so as not to send up their own satellite and have it bump into something on one of its orbits — they check the computer measurements back and forth through the centuries. Finally it came to a sudden halt when the computer stopped and put up a red signal, they knew that there was something wrong. They called the service department to check on the trouble, and they could not find nothing wrong on that end, and there was nothing wrong with the computer. But it kept refusing to go another day, which told them that there was a day missing somewhere down the line. Help me.

They began to scratch their heads but could not find the answer. They all agreed that there was a day missing in space and in the elapse of time, but what became of that day was the answer they sought. One of the men walked in one morning with his BIBLE in his hand.

"What's that?" his fellow workmen (the ones he went to Sunday school with) asked him.

"This is the BOOK and if the answer is not in this BOOK, the answer cannot be found."

So they began to search for the answer to the missing day in the BIBLE. They came to the book of JOSHUA and the tenth chapter and the eighth verse, and they found that Joshua was surrounded by the enemies, and the sun was almost down. If darkness fell, the enemies would overpower them in the night.

So Joshua asked the Lord to give him a little more time. God stopped the sun and made it stand still for almost a whole day. So the spacemen said, "Now there is the missing day."

But the Bible student said, "No, not completely. This was not a whole day but almost a whole day. But BRING ME THE BOOK. The answer is in the book."

So they began to search the book again and came to 2 Kings 20:9-11 and found where Hezekiah on his death bed was visited by the Prophet Isaiah who told him that he was not going to die (so set your house in order). But Hezekiah did not believe him and asked for a sign as proof. Isaiah said do you want the sun to move forward ten degrees, and he said no, but back ten degrees. Now ten degrees is exactly 40 minutes. So the 23 hours and 20 minutes delay in Joshua time, plus the 40 minutes in Hezekiah's time, made up the missing 24 hours.

LISTEN. WHATEVER WE NEED, WE FIND THE ANSWER IN THE book.

Just Remember WHATEVER IT IS, IT'S IN THE

BOOK!

"Do not let this BOOK of the Law depart from your mouth, meditate on it day and night, so that you may be careful to do everything written in it. They will be prosperous and successful." (Joshua 1:8)

"Afterward, Joshua read all the words of the law – the blessings and the curses – just as it is written in the BOOK of the law." (Joshua 8:34)

"So the sun stood still and the moon stopped till the nation avenged itself. Or nation triumphed over its enemies as it is written in the BOOK of life. The sun stopped in the middle of the sky and delayed going down abound Day." (Joshua 10:13)

"If you do carefully follow all the words of this law, which are written in this BOOK and do not revere this glorious and awesome name the LORD your God." (Deuteronomy 28:58)

The Presence of Christ in His Church

"The Lord is there." Ezekiel 40:35

Far more valuable to the church of Jesus Christ is that Divine presence here promised, than was the sacred Shekinah to the ancient people. The latter was only a mere symbol, once a year beheld by one man, but the former is a gracious power to be appreciated and felt by every true Christian heart. *"God is in the midst of her, the Lord is there."*

The Lord from His temple, looks upon the city and through the city to the whole land. It is the presence of Jesus Christ in the midst of His church that is here indicated.

His Observant Presence

Jesus is with us "always." (Matthew 28:20) Not in the body, but in the spirit and His spiritual presence, His observation of our inner life and of our outward conduct in the homes in which we live and in the different spheres in which we live and as well as when we are gathered together in His house or around His table. The near presence of our Lord is a thought, which should preserve us from folly and from sin, which should urge us to duty and to kindness, which should sustain us in trouble and in loss.

His Sympathetic Presence

We have need of His presence at all times, but we realize our need more especially and more profoundly in the time of our affliction. It is then that we feel the need of a Divine friend and an all-powerful deliverer.

Man fails us then. He may be something, or even much to us, but he leaves much to be desired and to feel that "the Lord is there" in the midst of our trails of life, in the anxieties of our daily duties in the pressing problems and sacred struggles of the church, means much to the mind of a devout Christian. In Jesus Christ, we have a present, sympathizing friend who enters into our sorrows, who goes down with us into the deepest waters through which we have to wade. Lifeguards in deep water call for help.

His Active Presence

Christ is with us, not only observing us and fencing for us, but also acting graciously upon us and through us.

By illuminating our minds by the inspiration of his holy spirit.

By sustaining our spiritual life by divine communications of power.

By responding to our devotion, accepting our praise, our adoration, hearing and answering prayers.

By energizing and effectuating our words to be "might" to pull down and to build up. The near presence of Christ should be the most powerful incentive to the pursuit of spiritual worth and to the execution of all

Christian enterprises.

THE CHRIST OF THE PRESENT, A FORETASTE OF FUTURE

Do not indulge in a vain regret. It would have been very pleasant to "see the Lord" as His apostles saw Him. To look into His face, to hear His voice and very honorable it would have been to minister to his necessities as THEY were permitted to do. But we can in fact and in truth be as near to Him now as they were then. For still, we listen to His word, and still, we serve Him. For inasmuch as we show kindness or render help to "one of these little ones," we do the same thing unto Him.

Do not cherish an unfounded hope. Many are the souls that lived and died disappointed, expecting to have a visible, present Savior among them.

The Devil is out to Get You

"And the Lord said, Simon, Simon, Simon, behold, Satan hath desired to have you, that he may sift you as wheat: But I have prayed for thee, that thy faith fail not. And when thou art converted, strengthen thy brother." Luke 22:31-32

In dealing with this passage of scripture, Jesus had been or was teaching the Apostles about their future reward in the future Kingdom. In verses 28 through 30 of this chapter, we find Jesus encouraging and instructing His followers.

For He saith, "Ye are they who have continued with me in my trials. And I appoint unto you a Kingdom as my father hath appointed unto me. That ye may eat and drink at my table in my Kingdom, and sit on thrones judging the twelve tribes of Israel."

But then Jesus made a special statement unto Peter, "Simon, Simon, behold, Satan has desired to have you, that he may sift you as wheat." The devil is out to get you. Well, the devil is out to get whoever He can. He is after all strong believers in Christ.

Jesus is saying to Simon Peter, "The devil desires to test you. He desires to tempt you. His aim is to trick you or cause you to fall." Peter was unable to see this and so are we. But the Lord Jesus does see him as he goes about; and He not only sees him, He can look into his heart and discern the secret purpose and desires of Satan.

Jesus was saying to Peter, "Peter! The devil want you! And you especially you. Believers in me, the devil is out to get you. Peter, you believe in me rather than in the Jews or heathen around you; you, my most beloved disciple. You, one with great self-confidence — you, who said by the Spirit of God, 'Thou art the Christ, the son of a Living God.' The devil is after you.

"First of all, Peter, He wants to make you a lie. He wants to make you claim that you don't know me." Listening to what Jesus said, the Pharisees were blind to the truth. John 8:44 says, "Ye are of your father the devil, and the lusts of your father you will do. He was a murderer from the beginning and abode not in the truth, because there is no truth in him."

When he speaketh a lie, he speaketh of his own. For he is a liar, and the father of it. I come to warn us, be careful and be strong, because the devil is out to get us!

We see that we are to regard our temptations as coming from Satan, the tempter and the accuser. He who rebelled against God in Heaven seeks to overthrow God's will and His Kingdom on Earth.

In tempting us, Satan takes advantage of two circumstances. He employs the world to seduce us, and he addresses the corruption of the heart. He takes advantage of the circumstances in which we are placed, and of the worldly and sinful character of those with whom we mingle.

It is of vast importance that Christians should know wherein the secret of their strength lies. It lies first of all in the intercession of Christ, and secondly in our faith in Jesus. Our strength is primarily not in self. It is not in the liveliness of our feeling on strength of resolutions.

For the purposes formed in our strength are like the writing upon the sand, which is swept away in the first breath of the tempest, on the first swelling of the tide. Our strength to withstand the power of Satan is in Christ.

James 4:7 says, "Submit yourselves, therefore, to God. Resist the devil, and he will flee from you." In order to escape the devil, we must draw near to God. For the devil is out to get you. The devil has no respect of person. He will try anybody.

He tried to get Joseph, but he failed. He tried to get Paul before he was converted. He tried John the Baptist but still failed. The devil is out to get all Christians to turn from the ways of righteousness. The devil is trying his best to tear down the Kingdom and the Church of God.

1 Peter 5:8 warns us, for it says, "Be careful, (sober) watch out for attacks (vigilant) from Satan, because your adversary, the devil, like a roaring lion, walketh about, seeking whom he can tear apart (devour)." The devil will try to separate the pastor from the church. The devil is out to get the choir in confusion.

The devil makes folks think can't nobody head and sing like them. The devil is out to get the deacons of the church. Satan makes them feel like they are there to control the church, the monies, and the pastor. Don't fool yourself, Brethren. The church was left in the hands of the preachers. I come to warn us that the devil is out to get us.

Wives, the devil is out to get you. Husbands, the devil is out to get you too. Family, Satan is out to rip you apart and to cause you to suffer the afflictions of this world. Listening to the devil caused man's first and only problem.

Genesis 3:4-5 says, "And the serpent said unto the woman, ye shall not surely die; for God doth knoweth that in the day ye eat thereof, then your eyes shall be open, and ye shall be as God, knowing good and evil." The devil doesn't pick certain people to try a test on. For the devil is so bold that he even tried Jesus Himself.

"And when he had fasted forty days and forty nights, he was afterward hungry. And when the tempter came to him, he said, 'If thou be the Son of God, command that these stones be made bread.' But he answered and said, 'It is written, Man shall not live by bread alone, but by every word that proceedeth out of the mouth of God.'" (Matthew 4:2-3)

The devil has some power. But Jesus has all power in Heaven and in Earth. Here is implied Peter's ignorance and present unadvisedness. He was not aware of this attempt of Satan. So is it likewise with many others of God's servants. Satan does secretly lay siege unto our soul, and many times we are unable to discern it.

It is great knowledge and skill for us to know when we are tempted, and to be apprehensive that we are under temptation. Peter was for real. Peter was a believer. Peter's faith was strong. Peter did not believe in taking junk! For He had said to Jesus, at one time. From Luke 22:33, "And he said unto him, 'Lord, I am ready to go with thee both in prison and to death.'"

But what Peter did not know is that the devil was waiting on just a few hours away. The devil would sting him in his flesh. What Peter did not understand was that man will fail under pressure.

Pressure will get next to you. What Peter did not know was that when a man seems to be under pressure of defeat, a man will change his mind.

Pressure will make you take down. Pressure will make you give up! Jesus said to Peter, "Peter the devil desires to have you, but I have already prayed for you, that your faith fail not." Just a few hours passed by, and they took Jesus and led him away, and brought him unto the high priest's house.

And Peter followed afar off. And when they had kindled a fire in the midst of the court, and were seated together, Petr sat down among them.

There was a maid that said, "This man was also with him."

But Peter denied him, saying, "Woman, I know him not."

And there were other witnesses that said they saw him. But Peter declared, "Man I am not one of them."

And there was a space passed, about an hour, and others said, "This fellow is also with him; for he is a Galilean."

But Peter spoke and said, "I know not what thou saith."

Pressure will make you deny the truth.

Not only Peter, but the devil is out to get us. He is out

trying to destroy the Church of Jesus Christ! The devil is out trying to discourage every strong Christian. He's out to destroy the believers in Christ. His desire is to conquer the Christian world.

But those of us who are strong in the Lord, let us hold to the author and finisher of our faith. For only the strong survive. Only the pure in heart shall see God. Therefore, let us sing with a strong conviction; you can't make me doubt him, no matter how you try; you can't make be doubt him. I know too much about him.

Although Satan is out to get us, let us be of good courage. Let us be strong in the Lord. For Satan was out to get Job. He went to Job, and stripped him of his earthly possessions. The devil took seven thousand sheep, three thousand camels, five hundred yoke of oxen, and five hundred she-mules.

The devil took all ten of Job's children. And then caused Job to be afflicted. But Job cried out, "Naked came I out of my mother's womb, and naked I shall return. The Lord gave, and the Lord hat taken away; blessed be the name of the Lord." Out of all this, the devil was defeated.

Yes, the devil is out to get us, but let us hold to our first love. Let us keep on praying! Let us keep on believing! Keep on trusting, keep on waiting, keep on running, keep on looking unto the hills, for our help is in the Lord. Our hope is in the Lord. For Jesus is out to get us also.

"Behold I stand at the door and knock; if any man hear my voice and opens the door, I will come in to him, and will sup with him, and he with me." (Revelation

3:20) Jesus is out to get us. For He defeated sin and death for our cause.

Let's fight the good fight, for the battle is not ours — it belongs unto the Lord. For Jesus said, "Lo, I am with you always, even unto the end of the age."

Don't let the devil ride. If you let him ride, he will want to drive. Let Jesus control your life, and let the Holy Spirit direct your faith!

Do You Have Reservation?
(This Sermon created for use at Funerals)

"But now thus saith the Lord that created thee, O Jacob, and he that formed thee, O Israel, Fear not: for I have redeemed thee, I have called thee by thy name; thou art mine. When thou passest through the waters, I will be with thee; and through the rivers, they shall not overflow thee; when thou walkest through the fire, thou shalt not be burned; neither shall the flame kindle upon thee. For I am the Lord thy God, the Holy One of Israel, thy Saviour." Isaiah 43:1-3a

"Let not your heart be troubled: ye believe in God, believe also in me. In my Father's house are many mansions: if it were not so, I would have told you. I go to prepare a place for you, I will come again and receive you unto myself; that where I am, there ye may be also. And whither I go ye know, and the way ye know. Thomas saith unto Him, Lord, we know not whither thou goest; and how can we know the way? Jesus saith unto him, I am the way, the truth, and the life: no man cometh unto the Father, but by me." John 14:1-6

    1. Read the texts above.
    2. Remarks of consolation to the family…
    3. One eulogizes his/her own funeral. We have come to celebrate the home-going of the deceased, (fill in the name).
    4. The Scriptures that were read in your hearing

affirm the fact that God, indeed, is our Creator and Redeemer. Each of us lives between the beginning and the end of a lifespan in this world. Being born in sin and shaped in iniquity, God gave His Son to redeem those who would be saved from the wrath to come, and all along the road of life, bless us relative to our needs. Christ Jesus is God's Way and Means Committee, by which we may be saved and get our reservation for Heaven.

5. This life is filled with many swift transitions. The valleys are low, the hills are high, and we must cross many rough places. Nevertheless, we hate to leave this world. But the death angel makes it so—we are here today and gone today. If man could invent something to perpetuate life here, I imagine some would try to live here forever. But God has fixed it so we must vacate this house of clay and move to another place. The body must return to the dust from which it came, and the soul must return to our Creator who gave us our being.

6. The Bible says, "It is appointed unto men once to die, but after this the judgment. So Christ was once offered to bear the sins of many and unto them that look for him shall he appear the second time without sin unto salvation. (Hebrews 9:27-28) So, all of us have an appointment with our destiny, and having a right relationship with God makes the difference as to where our souls shall spend eternity. Only through Jesus can one get reservation to eternally live with the Father.

7. One thing about the mystery of death is it is the most democratic thing that everyone equally shares. No

matter how wealthy, healthy, or otherwise we may be, we might as well start packing to make the journey to our eternal destiny. No wonder the psalmist said, "Lord, teach us to number our days, that we may apply our hearts unto wisdom." The wisdom of it all is we should already be packed, living each moment with His face in view. The wisdom of it all is to know Jesus in the pardon of our sins and live a prepared life. We do not know the hour that the Lord shall return, but we do know, according to His promise, He's coming again with judgement in His hands. But as long as you have gotten your business fixed with Jesus, you have a confirmed reservation. The Lord said those whose good exceeds their bad shall receive a just reward. In order for one's good to exceed the bad, he must know Jesus in the pardon of his sin.

8. The glorious thing about having salvation through Jesus Christ is when we accept Him as Saviour and Lord of life, and serve him to the best of our ability, He lets His mercy and grace balance the scales of justice, that He may take us home to live with Him forever. When we stand before our God, we want to hear Him say, "Well done." To hear Him say that, it must be well with our soul. Jesus is the only soul-fixer who is able to save us, keep us from falling and present us faultless before the throne of Grace. When He gives you reservation, He will surely see you through!

9. As we see the road ahead fastly becoming the road behind us, it behooves us to come into a right relationship with God. For one day, at the name of Jesus,

every knee shall bow and every tongue shall confess. Our good standing with our Creator and Redeemer depends on having Christ Jesus as Saviour and Lord. All along life's busy way, all of us do some good and some bad. The glorious part of it all is just as we are, without one plea, we can come to Jesus and He will save us. He will have mercy and abundantly pardon.

10. So, the crux of it all is in order to have reservation, one must first have Jesus. Heaven is a prepared place for prepared people, and only Jesus can give us safe passage into eternal joy with Him. It's my prayer and it's my hope that the deceased got his business fixed and confirmed his reservation with Jesus. It's my prayer and it's my hope that the rest of us will be ready when He comes. My mind is made up, and my heart is fixed to stay ready, as I live, move and have my being in Christ. I have my reservation confirmed, because Jesus fixed it for me a long time ago.

11. I came to Jesus, just as I was, a poor, weary sinner, in search for my Redeemer. And when I found Him, He let me know that He was in search for me, that He might save my soul and make me whole. Now I have reservation with my ticket stamped SAVED BY GRACE. Has Jesus confirmed your reservation? If you really want to cherish the memory of the deceased, start by insuring that you have a right relationship with God. Whatever he didn't do to your liking, you try to do it in a more excellent way. Whatever he did to your liking, carry it on in his memory.

12. Let me close by telling you a story about two men

who were traveling from Florida to New York. The flight was to stop in Washington, D.C. One man got booked to D.C., while the other man got a through reservation. When they arrived in D.C., they were required to change to another plane that was going to New York. They went by the ticket office to find that it was closed.

The first man said, "I won't be able to continue with you on the journey because I don't have a reservation on the plane."

The other man said, "Well, I have my reservation, and I am able to continue my journey home."

13. Church, that's what the Lord will do for you when He redeems you. He gives you a through reservation, and safe passage. He has conquered death, hell and the grave, making the grave just a stop-over. When you have reservation with Jesus, you are able to continue all the way through. From there, you shall be changed, from mortality to immortality! If you have your reservation, you need not let your heart be troubled. Just be ready when Jesus comes. Surely, he is coming again to receive you, that where he is, you, along with other believers, may be also. But you've got to have your reservation.

Do you have your reservation?

Gideon

Lord can save the people. We use force for war, need strength for self.

Text: Judges 6-7

Hiding out is a horrifying experience. Gideon and the Israelites had been driven from their homes and were forced to reside in caves, cliffs and temporary tents. As they had done frequently in their past, the Israelites had rebelled against God. Now, as was the pattern following such disobedience, they were under the threat of a foreign power. This time it was the Midianites.

The Midianites would run people from their homes and livestock. The Israelites resorted to living like fugitives in their own land.

One day while Gideon was threshing wheat to make bread, an angel of the Lord came to him and said, "The Lord is with you, mighty warrior!"

Gideon's response was very human. "But sir, if the Lord is with us, why has all this happened to us?"

This was a good question. Of course, the angel meant "now," not prior to deliverance.

One of the first things Gideon did was to offer a sacrifice to the Lord. Next, he broke down the Asherah pole. This was an object, which symbolized the goddess

Asherah, a female counterpart to Baal. He also smashed the altar of Baal. During this time of idol worship, such an act was punishable by death. Instead of killing Gideon, the people waited to see if Baal would kill him. Baal did not, because Baal was not a real god.

Gideon was unsure about Israel's immediate future. He asked for a sign from God about the salvation of Israel. Gideon took a fleece and laid it on the ground. He asked God to let the dew fall on the fleece, but not on the ground. This would be a sign that God would save Israel from its enemies.

The next morning it was just as Gideon had asked. He apologized and asked God to once again answer the test. This time Gideon asked that the fleece be left dry while the ground would be wet from the dew. The next morning it was so. When he saw the dry fleece, the one from which he had squeezed a bowlful of water the previous morning, he knew God was with him.

This was much more than an answered prayer—it was an invitation from God to deliver the people from the hands of the Midianites. Gideon's experience of God was unique but very natural. Although he questioned God twice in his use of a fleece, God did not punish him but instead recognized Gideon's doubt and proved to Gideon that he would be with him in this encounter.

When Gideon took the three hundred men to face the Midianites, he was full of confidence. His faith was at a high. He had never experienced God's presence more at any time. As they blew their trumpets, they not only experienced the deliverance of Israel, they experienced the glory of God.

PREPARE TO MEET GOD

1. What is God's way to win victory for his people? 7:1-25
2. Why do God's ways often create envy and jealousy among people? v1
3. What does God do to quiet human jealousy and provide hope and meaning? v3
4. Why do humans not always respond to God's ways? v5-7
5. What is God's way of dealing with those who do not join in his work? v7-9

DID YOU NOTICE?

1. God can work with a people who are not united to accomplish his work. v23:1-5
2. God does not want jealous and proud people. 7:23, 8:3
3. God uses people of faith, not certainty. v1-3
4. God does not honor people who try to remain neutral until they are sure of who is on the winning side. v13-17

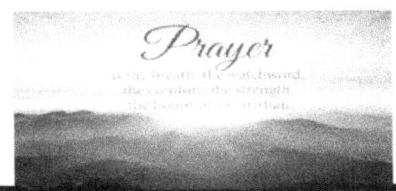

God is our refuge and strength, a very present help in trouble.
Psalms 46:1

For God sent not his Son into the world to condemn the world; but that the world through him might be saved. John 3:17

Tidbits to Make you Think, Smile or Laugh Out Loud

Some Favorite Sayings

I'm making like I am doing alright.

If I had your hand, I would throw mine in.

I am trying to make it in this world of yours.

When people are nice, they don't have to be nice to you.

I will bless the Lord at all times. His praise shall continually be in my mouth.

Hast thou not known? Hast thou not heard? The everlasting God, the Lord, the Creator of the end of the earth, fainteth not, neither is weary.

Nothing shall be able to separate us from the love of God, which is in Christ Jesus our Lord.

Stories

When I was growing up, we had a cat that wouldn't eat nothing but meat. My mother said, "Take him down the road and leave him there."

After about two weeks, the cat came back poor.

And Mama say, "Take him back. He won't eat bread—just meat.

The cat said, "I'll eat it now."

A Fisherman Tail

One day I went fishing at a lake in Texas. The weather was perfect, hardly any wind or waves on the water. I baited my hook with a big old shiner minnow and threw it way, way, way w---ay out there.

Then I tightened up my line and propped my rod and reel up on some rocks. After about 20 minutes, my line started to move, and the tip of my rod bent down. I grabbed it and pulled back hard to set the hook. I knew right then it was a big one!

He pulled this way and that way. I'd reel in 10 foot of line, and he'd pull out 15. We went back and forward for about 25 or 30 minutes. Finally I had him worn out. And I'm not lying, this was the biggest catfish the world has ever seen. In fact, when I pulled him out, the water in the lake dropped two feet.

When Coolade was about 10 or 12, his family had a fence around their yard. One day a man from the appliance rental store came to repo their TV, and Coolade was on the front porch when he showed up.

The man walked up to the fence and asked, "Is your mother home young man?"

"Yes, sir," he replied.

After a brief moment of silence, he said, "Well, may I speak with her?"

Coolade quickly answered, "No sir, and you ain't getting' our TV either."

The man smiled and decided to make small talk to

get on Coolade's good side. He looked around and saw that Coolade's dog had some puppies.

The man said, "Wow, your dog has ten puppies."

Coolade answered quickly again. "Well, if she has ten tits, she can have ten pups."

The man, getting a little frustrated, said, "Well, you know they're just mutts, don't you?"

Again Coolade answered quickly. "The momma dog is a mutt and the daddy dog is a mutt, so the pups are mutts too!"

Now the man is furious and blurted out, "There is not much between you and a fool, is there?"

Coolade looks him in the face and said, "No sir, only this here fence!"

My best friend's name is Coolade. We grew up together and have been friends from day one. No matter what the problem, we are there for each other. Like the time Coolade's woman left him for another man. That's right—another man. Coolade couldn't eat, couldn't sleep. He kept calling my house asking to speak to her. Man it was terrible.

A Few Jokes

A man walks into a Catholic church and asks the priest if he could have a funeral for his dog in his church.

The priest replies, "Sorry for your loss, but we don't hold mass for dogs."

So the man walks down the street to a Methodist

Church and asks the minister there if he could have his dog's funeral at his church.

The minister replies, "Sorry, sir, we don't perform funerals for dogs."

So the man walks on down the street until he sees a preacher sitting on the steps of a Baptist church.

The preacher sees that the man is bothered and asks, "Is everything alright young man?"

The man answers, "You wouldn't happen to perform funerals for dogs at your church, would you?"

The preacher kind of smiled and says, "No sir, we sure don't."

The man, looking very disappointed, says, "No one will funeralize my dog, and I even have $5,000 to spend on it."

The Baptist preacher stands up and replies, "$5,000! Will you be needing the choir to sing on that mournful day?"

A farmer's wife asked him to get rid of a dog of theirs that kept digging up the yard and tearing up any and everything it could. So the farmer loaded up the dog and drove about 20 miles away and left him there.

On the way back, he decided to call his wife to see if she needed anything while he was out. So he called home, and when she answered, he asked if she needed anything.

She said, "Yes I do. I needed you to come get this dog. He's back here chewing up my rosebushes."

So the farmer goes home and loads the dog up again.

This time he takes him about 30 miles away and leaves him.

On his way home, he decides to call his wife to see if she might want a burger or something to eat. So he called home and asked if she wanted something to eat.

She said, "No, I want you to come get this dog. He's back out there tearing up the garden.

So the farmer goes home and loads the dog up again and takes him 50 miles away, but this time he drives around and around and around to make sure the dog was lost and left him.

On the way home, the farmer called his wife. When answered, he said, "Baby, is that dog back at the house?"

She said, "Yes, he's over digging up the yard."

He said, "Good. Tell him to come get me because I'm lost!"

Sermons by Fellow Laborers
(used by permission – bios included where provided)

Unfounded Accusations
Sermon by Rev. Sinclair Royal, II

Matt. 27:11-14; Luke 23:2-5

There has to be an element of truth in any accusation brought against the defendant for a court to bring him to trial. Actual or circumstantial, the evidence against the defendant must be founded on truth. The witnesses' stories have to jive. Unfounded accusations cannot be used to indict or convict any defendant. However, there was a case, two thousand years ago, in which unfounded accusations did indict and convict. And that case was the one brought against the Lord Jesus Christ.

Matt. 27:11-14, Luke 23:2-5:

Let your mind drift with me for one moment. Let it drift back down the corridors of time. That's it, drift back to Pilate's courtroom, where our Lord and Savior will be convicted by unfounded accusations. See the Master as He stands alone before Pilate and his accusers. No mother or father by His side. Mary Magdalene isn't there. Lazarus, nor his sisters, are there. Even his favorite disciples have deserted Him. He stands alone to face unfounded accusations.

There is something ennobling, vindicating about undeserved suffering. It lifts the sufferer above his tormentors. Somehow, that person's stature is increased. Undeserved suffering has a way of immortalizing. Ask Martin Luther King, Jr. if you don't believe me!

Oh, it's one thing to get your just desserts, everybody agrees. An unfaithful husband caught in the throes of passion with an unclad "hoochie-mamma" deserves to be taken to the cleaners in Judge Judy's court. A backstabbing friend caught in the act of scandalizing a good friend's name should be whipped within an inch of his/her life with a barbed wire strap. A disobedient child determined to use Mamma's new sofa for a trampoline, after countless scoldings, ought to be strung up by his Tommy Hilfiger's. And a criminal caught red-handed at the scene of the crime ought to do mandatory time.

In each aforementioned case, the culprit deserves what they get—but not Jesus. He deserves none of what the Chief Priest's unfounded accusations will bring him. He stands before Pilate and the world guiltless and sinless. The accusations being lodged against Him are unfounded. The witnesses against Him couldn't even get their stories straight. There isn't even any corroborating evidence. Yet, here He stands, expected to cop-a-plea. He is made sin for our sakes.

See Jesus as He stands mute before Pilate while the Chief Priest assaults Him with a barrage of accusations. Amid the onslaught of vicious accusations, the slings and arrows of slander, and the downpour of outright lies, He stands unmoved. He refuses to play their games. He never says a mumbling word.

Why? Because He has already submitted to the

Father.

Remember the dark night in Gethsemane, when He went on a way's ahead of his three favorite disciples to pray? Sweat ran down His brow like blood as He wrestled with the fate of mankind. It was that night after begging the Father to spare Him the cross. He realized that He must die. Then in the peace of resolve, He says, "Father, not my will, but Thy will be done."

He was saying, "Lord, I'll go to whatever extremes you need me to go, I'll go. If it means being lied on, I'll go. If it means being scandalized, I'll go. If it means being totally dissed, I'll go. I'll go because the world needs to see what being fully committed to Your will means."

Lord God today. Had it been us, the Lord would have had to find somebody else. We would have been slinging snot, cussing, citing law statutes, and demanding to see Johnny Cochran. But not Jesus. He yielded His will to the Father's will. That's why He stands before Pilate, because He is fully committed.

What a Savior! The beauty of it is that He didn't only not stoop to their level, but indicted them with His manner. For when He does open His mouth, there is no opening argument, no torching defense, no torrid cross-examination. Life on the line and He upsets the apple cart with two words:

"Thou sayest..."

What a mighty God we serve! As he used parables to spellbind all but the elect, so how does He spellbind His accusers with two words? He mocks them.

"Thou sayest..."

Nothing else. Just, "Thou sayest…"

They thought He was agreeing with them, but He wasn't. He said one thing, but meant something else. He was really saying, "It is as you say, but not as you mean." God-a-mighty!

Break it down. He made His case with the connotative meaning of two words. Listen to the argument: "You say I'm the Christ. That is true. You say I've come to violently overthrow the Roman Empire as the Warrior King. That is not true. I come as the "Suffering Servant," not the "Warrior King." I won't come as the "Warrior King" until my second coming. You see, I've come as what you need, not as what you want."

He understood He had to die. None of the Jews understood this. Not even Judas and his zealot buddies. Had they understood, they wouldn't have tried to force Jesus' hand. He had to die. His life would only find its ultimate meaning in sacrifice. Full commitment had not only brought Him to this recognition, but to this acceptance. Calvary was a willing sacrifice for Him. He understood.

It's always man that gets it mixed up. Even today, we are still getting it mixed up. We've gotten salvation all mixed up. You know the argument of the two camps. One argues that the cross alone is the thing that brought us salvation. The other exclaims that Jesus Christ alone brought us salvation. But, both miss the mark. Salvation is the result of Jesus going to the cross, not either/or. Our salvation wasn't complete until He went to the cross. The cross without Jesus upon it makes salvation null and void. Had He not gone to the cross we'd still be lost.

Joel Gregory illustrates it like this: He asks how lightning is made. Most of his audience shake their heads, having forgotten the lesson of their 8th grade science class. Dr. Gregory then states that when warm, moist air with a positive charge collides with cold dry air with a negative charge, a cataclysmic reaction occurs and prickly fingered lightning flashes across a dark sky. His point is this—when the cold iron of the nails met the warm flesh of Jesus, a cataclysmic reaction occurred, and the prickly fingered lightening of salvation bolted across the dark skies of eternity--and my soul was saved. My salvation took Jesus and the cross. And in shame, I must admit that it took unfounded accusations to start the ball rolling.

You remember the story. Over 2,000 years ago, Jesus was made sin. He became sin for our sakes. He stood undaunted, unmoved, in the holding tank of eternity with true courage. Not the courage of retaliation, but the courage of sacrifice. He became our substitute. Scripture says, "Greater love than this hath no man..."

They marched Him before Pilate, deserted by all He loved. He stood there with the stateliness of a King, because He was the King of kings. To all their accusations, He never said a mumbling word. Since their unfounded accusations could not convict Him, nor their paid witnesses, they tried to use His silence against Him. They used it as evidence of His guilt.

You hear them don't you? "He doesn't speak because

He is guilty."

"Sick 'em Pilate."

But remember that undeserved suffering purifies, it ennobles. All Pilate could say after listening to all the evidence was, "I find no fault in him." Great-God-a-mighty!

If that's what Pilate said after Jesus refused to talk, imagine what he would have said had Jesus talked! Oh, God today, had Jesus talked. Had He talked, He would have gone scot-free. Had He talked, Pilate would have given Him clemency. His words would have condemned the prosecution.

Oh, yes, He could have talked.

He could have said: "Y'all need to check yourselves. The defenders of right shouldn't use unfounded accusations to make their case."

He could have said, "I move for an immediate dismissal on the grounds that wrong can't condemn right."

He could have said, "Look what you've done to my world!"

And He would have been perfectly in His rights because the Creator has the right to question the created. He could have even moved for an immediate dismissal on the grounds that the witnesses had been coerced. But, He didn't.

He didn't say any of these things. He sat through the Chief Priest's interrogation and never uttered a word. And then He sat through Pilate's only at the end uttering two words that turned the prosecution's case upside down. Then He shut up again because He knew He couldn't be exonerated.

He had to die.

Had Jesus not died, we'd still be lost in sin. Had He not died, the debt would still be unpaid. Had He not died, death would still have its sting and the grave have its victory. Without His death, there would be no atonement.

Thank God today that He died! He died, till the sun refused to shine. He died, till the moon dipped down in blood. He died, till my sins and yours were forgiven. He died, until the debt was paid.

And He said, "No charge!"

The Immutability of the God of Indemnity
By Rev. C.W. Fields

Malachi 3:1 "I am the lord, I change not."

This word immutability translated in the Greek is ametathetos, meaning unchangeableness. The perfection of God, by which He is devoid of all change in essence, attributes, consciousness, will and promises.

Before I get too far, I want to detoxify a face of God. There is no possible change in God. You can erase that thought from your mind. Theoretically, philosophically, scientifically, physiologically, psychologically, methodologically, anthropologically, archaeologically and act even theologically. There is no possible change in God.

The Jews made a miscalculation in looking for a Messiah to come and sit on a Jewish throne and destroy everybody else. But the ametathetos was accessible before there was ever a Jew in existence. The word Jew does not even occur before the period of Jeremiah, in the Old Testament. Originally, it denoted one belonging to the tribe of Judah, or to the two tribes of the Southern Kingdom. There is an account in 2 Kings 16:6 and 25:25. But later, its meaning was extended and it was applied to anyone of the Hebrew race who returned from captivity. Most of the exiles came from Judah and they were the main historical representative of ancient Israel. The term Jew finally came to comprehend all of the Hebrew race throughout the world.

In the second chapter of Matthew's Gospel, when Jesus was born, wise men came from the east asking "Where is He that is born King of the Jews." For we have seen His star and we have come to worship him." When King Herod, an earthly king, heard this he was troubled. Troubled because according to Genesis 25:6 and Judges 6:3, the men came from Arabia. Arabia is called the land of the East and the Arabians are called men of the East.

They came all the way from Arabia because they saw an extraordinary Person being born in the land of Judea. Because this star was over that land, in the nature of a comet or meteor and this differed so much from anything that was common, they concluded it to signify something uncommon. Their visit troubled Herod and all of Jerusalem.

Though Herod was king, he was an Edomite, not a Jew and it seemed like the Jews would have been rejoicing over a Jewish king being born.

We have expressed that there is absolutely no possible change in God, because all change must be to "better" or "worse" and God is absolute perfection. No cause for change in God. God exists, either in Himself or outside of Himself.

THE IMMUTABILITY OF GOD IS CLEARLY TAUGHT IN SUCH PASSAGES OF SCRIPTURE AS:

Psalms 102:26 *"The heavens shall perish but Thou shalt endure."* James 1:17 *"He is the Father of Lights with whom is no variableness neither shadow of turning."* Psalms 33:11 *"The counsel of the Lord standeth forever."*

The ametathetos of God must not be confounded with the Latin "immabilis" or the English "immobility," which means immoveable or unable to move. The immutability of God must not be confounded with immobility as if there were no movement in God. Immutability is consistent with constant activity and perfect freedom. God creates, performs miracles and sustains the universe. When the scriptures speak of His "repenting," as in Jonah 3:10, God didn't change. Try to remember that when God speaks on this wise, it's only an anthropomorphic way of speaking.

God adapts His treatment of men to the variations of their actions and character. When the righteous do wickedly, His holiness requires that His treatment of them must change.

The word "Malachi" means "messenger of Jehovah." Malachi is last of the Old Testament Prophets and author of the last book of the Minor Prophets. Nothing is known of Malachi but what his prophecy tells us. Ancient writers looked upon him as an angel incarnate. But many of the Jews believed him to be Ezra. Malachi's prominent message was the rebuke of the remnant and the announcement of future purging and blessing. The keynote of his book appears to be the unchangeableness of God and his unceasing love. The tone of his message is expostulation, blended with judgement. Yet, gracious promises and assurances are interspersed like pearls gleaming against a dark background. It's a mighty dangerous thing to bring charges against God. God does not immobilize robbery in the church. It's a deuced act to rob God and it takes a devilish person to even consider robbing Him today. Some of us feel that "What I have is mine" and "what I do with what's mine is my business" and will not accept the detergency of God.

The detergency of God.

I am led to believe that some of us profess to be saved and born again and yet we don't really know God is. Let me tell you something else about God. 1 Samuel 15:29 "and also, the strength of Israel will not lie, nor repent. For He is not a man that He should repent." The scriptures assert that God is absolutely without change. God does not change but He threatens that men may change. "It repented the Lord because He made man on the earth." God's character never changes but His dealings with men as they change from ungodliness to godliness and from disobedience to obedience.

The Holiness of God is the message to the entire Old Testament. In our world today when the awfulness of sin is so prevalent, we need a vision of His Holiness. When our churches are becoming immobilized and Family Prayer, at home has ceased and the chastening of children has vanished, we need a God of indemnity. INDEMNITY means security of exemption from damage, loss, injury or punishment. But, there was a man named Amos, who was a Judahite and the only thing we really know about Amos is that he had a son name Isaiah and an uncle name Uzziah. The Lord put His hands on Isaiah and this Prophet, Reformer and Write wrote a little Bible, bearing 66 chapters.

Sin had become so prevalent and men and women were "born in sin and shaped in iniquity." My grandparents sinned and my parents sinned and I sinned and YOU have sinned.

Oh Lord!

"Tell them He hath borne our griefs and carried our sorrows. Tell them He was wounded for transgressions, bruised for our iniquities and the chastisement of our peace was upon Him and with His stripes we are healed. Tell them that all we like sheep have gone astray. We have turned everyone to his own way and the Lord hath laid on Him the iniquity of us all." I don't know how, but Peter got the message in 1 Peter 2:24 *"Who his own self bare our sins in his own body on the tree, that we, being dead to sins, should live unto righteousness; by whose stripes ye were healed."*

Now, you can't talk about a Tree without talking about CALVARY.

On CALVARY, He was nailed to a cross between 9:00 am and 12:00 noon.

Between 3:00 pm and 4:00 pm HE DIED and He stayed in the grave THREE DAYS AND THREE NIGHTS Fighting Death. He made Death disabled and put Death in the Hospital.

Let Jesus Give you Rest*

"Martha, Martha, you are worried and troubled about many things." Luke 10:41

    Mary and Martha were two sisters who were as different as night and day. Martha was the picture of the perfect hostess. She loved to entertain company — of course, as long as they called in advance. If they had such magazines in her day, Martha certainly would have been a subscriber to Southern (Bethany) Living and Better Homes and Gardens. The Bible does not tell us, but perhaps her last name was even Stewart! Martha is a perfectionist and yet, she is her own worst enemy. She sets expectations that she can never meet. She is never able to completely rest and be content. Life for Martha is always an unfinished task.

    On the other hand, Mary, Martha's sister, is not much into the hostess scene.

    It's not that Mary does not also enjoy having company over, but Mary is more interested in conversation than the day's menu. When you drop in at Mary's house for a visit she may have you go fetch your own glass of iced tea. It's not that Mary doesn't care. Mary just takes life as it comes and material comforts and hostess graces are just not that important to her.

    It's easy to focus on Martha's apparent frustration

and anger, but I want you to consider her in a little different light. Martha is not really a bad person. In fact, she is a woman of dedication and she is a doer. I can just imagine that she is the kind of woman that probably seldom complains, seldom misses the smallest details, and she can always be counted on when you need her. Martha is certainly a commendable woman. Thank God for the Martha's of the world! This story is not in the Bible to teach us that serving is bad and that sitting is good. Under different circumstances serving may have been the best course of action.

Instead, this is a story about maintaining a much-needed balance in life. It's a story about the need to recognize that we are human. We stumble, and we fall short. It's a story about being human and how we desperately need to realize just how human we are. It's a story about setting priority and making the best choices in life. In life we are not usually confronted with choices that are outright good vs. bad! Those are the easy ones to make. But, oh how difficult are the everyday choices between what is good and what is best!

In this instance (Luke 10:38-42) there were more important things to do than housework and preparing supper. What Jesus desired was not dinner, but devotion. Martha was "worried and troubled about many things." Martha's worried and anxious heart would not find rest in serving (trying harder and doing more) but by sitting at the feet of Jesus and finding rest in His presence.

One time, when Jesus was at the home of Mary and Martha, Mary broke a very expensive bottle of fragrant perfume, and she anointed Jesus with oil (Mark 14:3-9, John 12:1-8). This was an expression of Mary's love and devotion to Jesus. Some of Jesus' disciples became infuriated at her for doing that. Martha was there (John 12:2) and I am certain that she too chimed in with the disciples in chastising Mary for her extravagance.

In Luke 10:38-42, we discover an occasion where the stark contrast between these two sisters, Martha and Mary, is obvious. Mary is sitting at the feet of Jesus. Martha is busy "with much serving." Mary is enthralled as she sits at the feet of the savior. Martha is enraged as she busily paces back and forth from the kitchen to the living room. The Bible tells us (Luke 10:38) that Martha welcomed Jesus into her house. This visit does not appear to have been planned. Because of the short notice there would be much work to do if dinner was going to be on the table. It did not take long for Martha to become stressed and angry at the fact that Mary was sitting while she was serving.

Martha directed her anger towards Jesus (Luke 10:40). She is essentially saying, "Lord, if you really cared about me you would rebuke my sister, Mary, and tell her to get in the kitchen."

Martha is ordering Jesus around and telling Him what to do! Anger, frustration and resentment often comes out in this kind of controlling way. When people do not act the way we want them to, we often want someone else to straighten the person out for us.

In Jesus Christ, we are set free from a life that seeks to only please others, and we are set free from a life of trivial pursuit and emptiness.

How about you? Is your life filled with purpose and peace? Or does your life look more like Martha's life—stressed and frayed?

When you accept Christ, then you are able to accept yourself and become empowered to accept others. There is good news for the "bedraggled, beat-up and burnt out!" That good news is that you can experience God's rest and acceptance today.

Where do you start? First, recognize that you are human. Like all humans we fall short (Romans 3:23). We cannot make it in life without Jesus Christ—His grace and power. Even Martha types need Jesus.

Second, give Jesus Christ complete control of your life. Simply said, don't try to be superwoman, (or superman for that matter) but let Christ give you His peace and rest. Jesus' words still ring true for us today: *"Come to me, all you who labor and are heavy laden"* (distracted) *and I will give you rest."*

*Note: This sermon was untitled when shared with the book editor/publisher.

Sense and Common Sense in a World of nonsense
PASTOR E. J. BALL, NEW FELLOWSHIP BAPTIST CHURCH, HOUSTON, TX

Text: 1 Kings 3:25-27
"And the king said, Divide the living child in two, and give half to the one, and half to the other. Then spake the woman whose the living child was unto the king, for her bowels yearned upon her son, and she said, O my lord, give her the living child, and in no wise slay it. But the other said, Let it be neither mine nor thine, but divide it. Then the king answered and said, Give her the living child, and in no wise slay it: she is the mother thereof."

Introduction

By the term, "in a world of nonsense," is meant a word that is characterized by a cold, selfish and indifferent attitude toward the fortunate and less fortunate people of the world—a world that lives or seeks to live on the "receiving end" of a balanced economic system of society. A world that lacks the moral and spiritual development, which characterize the dignity of a great people.

In such a world of nonsense, there is scarcely no interest in, nor sympathy for the unfortunate person on the other end of the scale—the one who is the "debtor" and all other such persons who fall into similar categories.

The slogan or order of the day, is an attitude such as: "Just so I get mine."

What happens to the other fellow, whether he drops dead, or his family starves or dies in the breadline after the bill is paid makes scarcely no difference at all. "Just so I get mine." What happens to the alcoholic, the dope fiend, or the wine-head, or to those families so gravely affected after such venoms are bought and the bill paid, makes no difference at all to those who push in such greed. "Just so I get mine" is the slogan.

This is largely, the spirit, which seems to underlie the basic structure of most of our present economic system today — a man's indifferent attitude toward man.

In a world of such nonsense, divining wisdom is the greatest modifier of mankind. The greatest thing that may be said of a man is that he is a wise man. It is greater than being rich or poor, white, yellow, brown, or black, large or small. It is that sort of thing that puts one on the top of that which is excellent. If one has such wisdom, those in a world of nonsense or affected by a world of nonsense will make a beaten path to his door.

Knowledge, Sense and Common Sense Analyzed

Let us think of wisdom as being divided into three parts, known as knowledge, sense, and common sense.

(a) In the first place, knowledge comes from without. It may be found in books, brooks, stones. It may be gotten from persons, personalities, places and things, or from any variety of related or unrelated phenomena. It is what one learns outside of himself.

(b) Sense comes from within. It is the capacity of one to learn or to know. It is the capacity of one to hold knowledge, or to hold what he learned from the things outside of himself. Sense is a response to the impulses of sensations that stimulate one to learn or to know. Sense is the vessel that holds knowledge. It is what one takes to school or college to put knowledge into, and knowledge is what he takes away from school.

(c) Common Sense comes from above—whereas, knowledge comes from without, sense comes from within, common sense comes from God.

When this writer was a child in the class of arithmetic, he was taught that common fractions had a numerator, a denominator, and that such fractions of great magnitude could be reduce to its lowest term by finding the least common denominator that would divide into all of the series of denominators above the line in sequence of the common fraction. Common sense is that sixth sense which keeps the other five natural senses from making fools of themselves.

Exposition

This text focuses on Solomon as he discerns a real mother from an imposter. The immediate importance of this text is reflected in its history. Solomon had become king of Israel ahead of his brother. There were many who accused him of being young and inexperienced, having risen to the throne only because he was the favorite son of King David who named and installed him as king before his death. The text focuses on one of many decisions Solomon made as king that was dramatic enough to demonstrate he was truly one wise enough to serve as king.

Two women both had infant children the same age and lived in the same quarters. During the night one of the women rolled over atop of her child and killed it. In the night, the mother of the dead child switched babies with the other. The switch discovered, the two women disputed each other's claim to the live baby. Their case came before Solomon, acting in his capacity as judge. He heard the claims of both women.

Obviously, one of the women was lying. The guilty mother faced certain death if she admitted to her part in the lie, so she continued her claim. Solomon decided to resolve the dispute by cutting the baby in half, giving one half to each. The guilty woman said that was a fair action. It was a matter of survival. At least she would not be slain or convicted in the process.

The real mother did not consider herself at all, but instantly threw herself before the king pleading for the life of the child. Her action immediately identified her as the real mother. Solomon gave her the whole baby uncut. The action established Solomon's wisdom in the mind and hearts of the people as it was repeated in their hearing.

The guilty woman had made a mistake. However, to cover her mistake and the error of her ways she was willing to destroy the life of an innocent child to insure her own survival. She took no thought of the life she would terminate — destroy the life of an innocent child to insure her own survival. She took no thought of the life she would terminate, only her own safety and well-being. To guarantee that safety she was willing to go half on a baby, especially since the baby involved was not her own and meant nothing to her. The baby was simply a means to achieve an end. The baby was a ticket to freedom. If cutting the baby in half could accomplish what she needed, then she was satisfied.

The real mother on the other hand had the concern of her child at heart. She would prefer to have a whole baby alive than half of a baby dead. She would prefer to see her baby alive and well in someone's care than to have only half a baby. That was the level of emotional commitment Solomon hoped his act would elicit—an outpouring of sympathy and love that would be unparalleled. When the appropriate time came, real love would be displayed, even at the expense of the mother's life. The guilty mother's disinterest in the welfare of the child represents the way the world receives every person—a means to achieve an end. Generally, Satan enters a life, uses it and tears it apart.

It does not matter to him whether a life is lost or ruined, only that his purpose is achieved. Much like the possessed man who ran naked through the graveyard and was not considered beyond how he could be used, so Satan destroys every life in which he can get a grip.

The real mother demonstrated God's love for his people. Not selfish in its intent, God's love moves men to raise themselves to higher levels of respect for life and well-being of others. In no way would God's love seek only half of a being. He seeks to preserve every part of His creation as a complete and whole being.

I. Suppose we take another look at sense

Sense is a natural response to the five senses of an organism. It is a response that is natural to the five sense of the animals of lower species of life. These animals, also, are born with five senses. They too, can see, hear, taste, smell and feel. Many of them have senses far keener than yours or mine. For instance, the dog can beat you smelling. The cat has a keener sense of feeling. The snake can beat you seeing in the darkness, and the eagle and dove have far stronger eyesight than we. And none of these creatures have to wear glasses.

It takes common sense to lift man above the level of these lower beasts and place him in the category just a little "lower than the angels." Thus man can't stop on the level of sense and be safe. Any person—adult or juvenile—who cannot control the impulses of his five senses is still on the level of the beast. He should have that sixth sense to lift himself. Common sense is that sixth sense which keeps the other five natural senses from making a fool out of themselves. In a world of nonsense, it is the sixth sense which keeps one from making a fool of himself.

Common sense involves planning ahead. When Jesus was teaching His disciples, He introduced this principle. He said, "Suppose one of you wants to build a tower. Will he not first sit down and estimate the cost to see if he has enough money to complete it?" (Luke 14:28)

Count the cost. That's another way of saying, "Plan ahead." Rushing headlong into projects, programs, or participation is worse than unwise. It's foolish. Naive haste, so common to youth, can speed us into troubles not easily undone. In fact, the gouges can leave permanent scars. That's hard to imagine, isn't it? We think things just ought to go smoothly. We don't usually anticipate problems. Much less do we expect some dreadful consequences.

Do you know what causes young adults to have this oblivious view of things? Zeal. That's right. It's the "I'm-gonna-change-the-world" syndrome. That headstrong eagerness can cause the bull to break a lot of dishes in the china shop.

Good common sense reminds us to sit down and think ahead. "What will be the results? Who will be affected? Is it worth it? Is it necessary? What does God think? So, common sense asks.

Charles Spurgeon said, "Zeal and discretion are like the two lions which supported the throne of Solomon. They make a fine pair but are poor things apart. Zeal without discretion is wildfire, and discretion without zeal is cowardice."

Discretion and zeal must basket-weave together. So, launch out! But be sure your boat is ready.

II. *Common sense involves simplicity.*

It lies deep in the bosom of basics. Enormous amounts of head-knowledge have little to do with common sense. Simplicity is the conveyor that carries profundity from one mind to the next.

Be basic. God uses the simple man far oftener than the worldly-wise man. I don't mean that you should be ignorant, nor uneducated, nor mediocre. No one who is capable of doing better should settle for "average." One does not have to be simple-minded to be simple. Just don't be too smart for your own good. Paul said there were some who professed themselves to be wise, but they had become fools. They outsmarted themselves.

Using forty-dollar words in fifty-gallon sentences may be impressive—and confusing. The Apostle John, always known for his plain way of saying things, used only three words to pen one of theology's most prominent truths. "God is love." (1 John 4:8) Bible scholars, over the centuries, have written tons of pages and googles of words on "God is love." But none said it better than John. Simplicity can never be outdone.

III. *Common sense involves not repeating the same mistakes.*

Charles Spurgeon created a fictional character named John Ploughman. Spurgeon used Ploughman as a pen name to write for "ploughmen, the common people"

Once he made Ploughman to say, "He who boasts of being perfect is perfect in folly. I have been a good deal up and down the world, and I never did see a perfect horse or a perfect man, and I never shall till two Sundays come together. You cannot get white flour out of a coal sack, nor perfection out of human nature; he who looks for it had better look for sugar in the sea."

All of us have a very vulnerable flaw of weakness—

mistake-making. We regret some things. We wish we could do things over again. We learn from them. We vow never to do them again. Then, when we least expect it, our hands tremble, our feet stumble, and out mouth mumbles. The same mistake has just been repeated.

We ask ourselves, "When am I going to learn my lesson?"

A common-sense person learns from mistakes, and won't make the same ones again. Why? For one, it isn't worth doing again. Second, obviously there's a better way. Lastly, in spite of the blunder, common sense learns what changes could be made to turn blemishes into beauty.

Let me close by saying:

...a WELL in the midst of a wilderness...
...a LIGHT in the midst of darkness...
...a REFUGE in the midst of storms...
...a FEAST in the midst of a famine...
...an OASIS in the midst of a desert...
...a CALM in the midst of violence...
...a PEARL in the midst of pebbles...
...a DIAMOND in the midst of dust...
...a SONG in the midst of sorrow...
...a LAMB in the midst of wolves...
...a DOVE in the midst of vultures...
...a VIRGIN in the midst of harlots...
...a ROSE in the midst of thorns...
...a GARDEN in the midst of a jungle!

Although it has been nearly 2000 years since Christ lived upon this earth, His life is STILL considered to be as...

...a JEWEL in the midst of junk...
...a RAINBOW in the midst of storm clouds...
...a FRAGRANCE in the midst of rottenness...
...a VICTORY in the midst of defeat...
...a FRIEND in the midst of enemies...
...a BLESSING in the midst of burdens...

The lily of the Valley!
Jesus, the bright and morning star!
Jesus, the sweet Rose of Sharon!
Jesus, the fairest of ten thousand!

Nobody but Jesus came down to the world...
He was born in Bethlehem!
He was raised in Nazareth!
He died in Jerusalem!

Jesus, who died on the cross until the sun in darkness hid itself. He died until God took a dagger and stabbed the moon, and she took the judgment hemorrhage and vanished away. He died until the little star, twinkling in the un-navigated other look at each other and saw no one shining but them, got ashamed of themselves, closed their dazzling eyes and fell like blasted figs and filled the earth with cosmic dark.

One Friday evening,
Went down in the grave,
Stayed there… all Friday night.
But early Sunday morning…
He got up from the grave with all power in His hands!
I have got all power!
All power! All power!
I have got all power, wrapped in my hand.

If Loving You Is Wrong, I Don't Want To Be Right
(ERRP Magazine Archives Of Sermon Of The Month)

"For God so loved the world that he gave his only begotten Son, that whosoever believeth in him should not perish, but have everlasting life." John 3:16

There is enough truth in that scripture to fill a thousand sermons. This is surely the greatest verse ever penned. All the great writings of the poets and sages of the entire world fall far short of the majestic sweetness contained in this one sentence. This verse has been called The Gospel in a Nutshell. It has been called the world's greatest love story. It has been called Christ's Gospel in one sentence. Every child in Sunday school knows this verse by memory and if everyone in the world acted upon this truth, the world would be transformed and all of us would be on the way to heaven.

God's love is shown in this verse. *"God so loved."* A sinful world is shown in this verse. *"God so loved the world."* The greatest gift is shown in this verse. *"He gave his only begotten Son."* The greatest privilege is shown in this verse. *"Whosoever believeth."* The greatest promise is shown in this verse *"should not perish, but have everlasting* life."

Love is one of the most bandied-about words in the English language. Flip on the radio, and there it is, the casual "I love you" from a call in listener to a radio announcer. I love deep-dish pizza commercial or the latest hit on the music charts. But loved defined as Paul understood it is quite another thing. Paul had in mind an action or attitude, how love behaves. (Notice how few words or phrases he used, each with its particular contribution.) Love, Paul might have said, is not that sentimental rush of warmth spawned by a moonlit night and the aroma of roses. Love continues when there is no moon at all. Love doesn't restrict itself to one person or even to one's family and friends. Whatever the circumstances and whatever the person, loves continue to express gentleness and humility, patience and courtesy.

Love continually waits for and seeks the best in others, never shoving for glory, never jealously wanting someone else's gifts. Love is on God's side, enduring as He endures, hoping for the best, believing that good will triumph in the end.

It has been said, "They who love are but one step from heaven. Love never asks how much must I do, but how much can I do? There are more people who wish to be loved, than there are willing to love. I heard a song the other day, and the words of this song did something to me. It disturbed my thinking.

The title of the song was, "If Loving You Is Wrong, I Don't Want to Be Right." I thought on the words to that song and began to write this sermon using the title as my subject. The words to the song talk about a desire to pursue a love between two people who aren't married to each other. In spite of the singer's status as a married man with two little children. It speaks of an unrighteous hunger, willing to see each other whenever they can as opposed to freedom to be together all the time. Basically, he wants to justify his needs to be with this woman that isn't his wife. And he has no concern about whether it is wrong. He wants the feeling more than the rightness. **

There are many loves, but no love like God's love. We have romantic love, we have physical love, and we have experimental love.

There is love of a citizen for his country.
There is love of a graduate for his school.
There is love of a sailor for the sea.
There is love of an astronomer for the stars.
There is love of a farmer for the farm.
There is love of a dreamer for adventure.
There is love of a scientist for the truth.
There is love of a poet for beauty.
There is love of a father for his son.

But Jesus says in John 15:13 *"Greater love hath no man than this, that a man lay down his life for his friends,"* None of these earthly loves are essential to salvation. Let us see if we can define the kind of love that John is talking about.

Mathematicians cannot figure it out. Historians cannot date its origin. Physiologists cannot reason it out, and geographers cannot locate its depth. Geometry cannot measure its height. The artist cannot paint its beauty. Photographers cannot take its picture. Physicians cannot diagnose it. Architects cannot blueprint it, sculptors cannot chisel it, carpenters cannot lay its foundation, and bankers cannot buy it.

The law cannot segregate it. Uncle Sam cannot ration it. The electrician cannot improve its light. The mastermind cannot understand it. The critics cannot deny it. The poor cannot desert it for they need it. And the politicians cannot vote it out of the hearts of Christians. Organizations cannot organize it out of the minds of saints. Scientist cannot bomb it out of existence. Fire cannot burn it. Swords cannot pierce it. Water cannot drown it. Beast cannot eat it up. Enemies cannot quiet it down, and the devil cannot stop its progress.

Daniel will tell you that God's love was the zookeeper in the lion's den. The three Hebrew boys will tell you that it was the everlasting love of God that acted as the fire chief in the fiery furnace. God's love fed Elijah in a famine. God's love gave strength to Moses and courage to Joshua. Noah will tell you that it was the love of God that caused him to build the Ark for the saving of sinners.

If you could check with Joseph, he would tell you that God's love brought him from a slave to a governor. God's love was the assurance in old age for Isaac, and the deliverance of Jacob. It was God's love that met Paul on the Damascus road and changed him from a persecutor to a preacher. In St. John 3:16 it says, *"For God so loved the world that he gave his only begotten Son, that whosoever believeth in him should not perish, but have everlasting life."*

** The actual words to the popular song were included in the sermon, but here it is paraphrased to avoid copyright infringement.

Men Ought Always Pray

Prayer Draws Us Closer to God

The answer to prayer is assured not only by the promises of God, but also by God's relation to us as a Father.

"But you, when you pray, go into your room, and when you have shut your door, pray to your Father who is in the secret place; and your Father who sees in secret will reward you openly." Matthew 6:6

Again, we have these words:

"If you then, being evil, know how to give good gifts to your children, how much more will your Father who is in heaven give good things to those who ask Him!" Matthew 7:11

Prayer Increases Confidence in Asking

God encourages us to pray, not only by the certainty of the answer, but also by the generosity of the promise, and the bounty of the Giver. How princely the promise!

"And whatever things you ask in prayer, believing, you will receive." Matthew 21:22

Then add to that "whatever" this promise: *"If you ask anything in My name, I will do it."* (John 14:14)

That verse covers all things, without qualification, exception or limitation. The word "anything" expands and makes specific the promise. The challenge of God to us is, *"Call to Me, and I will answer you and show you great and mighty things, which you to not know."* (Jeremiah 33:3) This includes, like the answer to Solomon's prayer (see 1 Kings 3:5-14) what was specifically prayed for, but embraces vastly more of great value and of great necessity.

Almighty God seems to fear we will hesitate to ask largely, apprehensive that we will strain His ability. He declares that He is *"able to do exceedingly abundantly above all that we ask or think."* (Ephesians 3:20) He almost paralyzes us by giving us a carte blanche, *"Ask Me of things to come concerning My sons; and concerning the work of My hands, you command Me."* (Isaiah 45:11)

How He charges, commands and urges us to pray! He goes beyond promise and says, *"God so loved the world that He gave His only begotten Son."* (John 3:16)

"He who did not spare His own Son, but delivered Him up for us all, how shall He not with Him also freely give us all things?" (Romans 8:32)

God gave us "all things" in prayer by promise because He had given us "all things" in His Son. What an amazing gift — His Son! Prayer is as immeasurable as His own blessed Son. There is nothing on Earth or in Heaven, for time or eternity that God's Son did not secure for us. By prayer, God gives us the vast and matchless inheritance that is ours by virtue of His Son. God charges us to *"come boldly to the throne of grace."* (Hebrews 4:16) God is glorified and Christ is honored by large asking.

Prayer Is a Part of God's Plan

What is true of the promises of God is equally true of the purposes of God. We might say that God does nothing without prayer. His most gracious purposes are conditioned on prayer. His marvelous promises in the 36th chapter of Ezekiel are subject to this qualification and condition. *"Thus says the Lord GOD, 'I will also let the house of Israel inquire of Me to do this for them.'"* (Verse 37)

In Psalm 2, the purposes of God to His enthroned Christ are enjoined by prayer. The decree that promises to Him the nations for His inheritance relies on prayer for its fulfillment. "Ask of Me." (Verse 8) We see how sadly the decree has failed in its operation, not because of the weakness of God's purpose, but by the weakness of man's praying. It takes God's mighty decree and man's mighty praying to bring to pass these glorious results.

In the 72nd Psalm we have an insight into the mighty power of prayer as the force that God moves on the conquest of Christ. *"Prayer also will be made for Him continually."* (Verse 15)

In returning, penitent sinner's prayer is based on a promise. The child of God's prayer is founded on his relationship to his heavenly Father. What the earthly father has belongs to the child for present and prospective uses. The child asks — the father gives. The relationship is one of asking and answering, of giving and receiving. The child is dependent on the father, must look to the father, must ask of the father and must receive of the father.

We know how with earthly parents asking and giving are inherent in the parent-child relationship and how in the very act of asking and giving, the relationship of parent and child is cemented, sweetened and enriched. The parent finds his wealth of pleasure and satisfaction in giving to an obedient child, and the child finds his wealth in the father's loving and continuous giving.

It must be kept in mind that there is no test of our being in the family of God that is surer than this thing of prayer. God's children pray. They rest in Him for all things. They ask Him for all things—for everything. The faith of the child in the father is evinced by the child's asking. It is the answer to prayer that convinces men not only that there is a God, but also that He is a God who concerns Himself about men and about the affairs of this world. Answered prayer brings God near and assures men of His being. Answered prayers are the credentials of our relationship to and our representation of Him. Men who do not receive answers to prayer from Him cannot represent God.

The possibilities of prayer are found in the unlimited promise, the willingness and the power of God to answer prayer, to answer all prayer, to answer every prayer and to supply fully the immeasurable needs of man. None is as needy as man—none is so able and anxious to supply every need and any need as God.

Prayer Is Powerful

Prayer affects God more powerfully than His own purposes. God's will, words and purposes are all subject to review when the mighty power of prayer comes in. How mighty prayer is with God may be seen as He readily sets aside His own fixed and declared purposes in answer to prayer. The whole plan of salvation would have been blocked had Jesus Christ prayed for the twelve legions of angels to carry dismay and ruin to His enemies. (See Matthew 26:53.)

The fasting and prayers of the Ninevites changed God's purpose to destroy that wicked city (see Jonah 3:1-10), after Jonah had gone there and cried unto the people, "Yet forty days, and Nineveh shall be overthrown!" (Verse 4)

Jesus Sets the Example in Prayer

Almighty God is concerned in our praying. He wills it, He commands it, He inspires it. Jesus Christ in Heaven is always praying for us (Hebrews 7:25). Prayer is His law and His life. The Holy Spirit teaches us how to pray. He prays for us *"with groanings which cannot be uttered."* (Romans 8:26)

All these examples show the deep concern of God in prayer. They reveal very clearly how vital prayer is to His work in this world and how far reaching are its possibilities. Prayer is at the very center of the heart and will of God concerning men. *"Rejoice always, pray without ceasing, in everything give thanks; for this is the will of God in Christ Jesus for you."* (1 Thessalonians 5:16-18)

Prayer is the polestar around which rejoicing and thanksgiving revolve. Prayer is the heart sending its full and happy pulsations up to God through the glad currents of joy and thanksgiving.

Prayer Brings Amazing Results

By prayer, God's name is hallowed. By prayer God's Kingdom comes. By prayer is His Kingdom established in power and made to move with conquering force swifter than light. By prayer, God's will is done until Earth rivals Heaven in harmony and beauty. By prayer, daily labor is sanctified and enriched, pardon is secured and Satan is defeated. Prayer concerns God and concerns man in every way.

God has nothing too good to give in answer to prayer. There is no vengeance pronounced by God so dire that does not yield to prayer. There is no justice so flaming that is not quenched by prayer.

Take the record and attitude of Heaven concerning Saul of Tarsus. That attitude is changed and that record is erased when the astonishing condition is announced, *"Behold, he is praying."* (Acts 9:11)

A Letter From the King
Sub-Topic: "The Christian Passport"

"Moreover I said unto the king, if it pleases the King, let a letter be given to the Governors beyond the river that they convey me over till I come to Judah." Nehemiah 2:7

Letter writing is one of the oldest arts in the knowledge of man. They have used it for many things and too many advantages. The best recognized authority any man can carry is a letter from the proper source. The letter from the right man will give authority to him who bears it.

Nehemiah was a servant in Shushan, in the palace of the King. After listening to the bad news of conditions of his old home, he wanted to go back and see if he could do something to help the condition. When the King saw how downcast he was, he inquired about the reason, and wanted to know if he could help in the matter.

"If it pleases the King, first a letter be given me to the Governors beyond the river that they may convey me over till I come unto Judah."

This letter was to serve as a passport and open the way for him to do his work. Anyone who expects to do business in a far country must have a passport, and it must be signed by the proper authorities. If he was to attain any object or reach any aim, the favor of the great, was his passport. In diplomatic circles, to receive a passport is to be dismissed from an enemy country. But to request one, it must come from the homeland.

Nehemiah was a member of two governments. One by adoption, and the other by birth. He wanted to pass from his home of adoption to the land of his birth in order to help rebuild the walls of the city, so it would be protected from its enemies. To do so, he requested a letter from the King. This letter was to the governors beyond the river that they might let him pass safely on his journey.

Nehemiah's letter of long ago, is the Christian's passport today. A Christian is a member of two countries, or two worlds. This present world, and the land across the river. The difference between present day Christian and Nehemiah is that Nehemiah was to do his word beyond the river, while the Christian has to do his work here. Nehemiah's letter had been requested, while the Christian has his already. It is signed and stamped by the King himself. Nehemiah's passport was signed in ink, while the Christian's passport is signed in blood. One represents time, while the other represents eternity.

Nehemiah wanted permission to pass through in order to get to the place where he was to do his work. But the Christian's passport is a permission of passage from the point of labor, to a place of rest.

It serves as a visa, or directive, to the authority along the way. It orders them to let you pass, and grants you what you want in order to make the journey safe and pleasant.

Nehemiah was interested in the land beyond the river because it was the homeland. The place of all his hopes and dreams, and too, his mother and father and all patriots of the past were sleeping and slumbering there. So when he heard the news about the condition over there, he wanted to go there himself. For more than two thousand years, news has been coming in from the country beyond the river to the Christian family, telling of conditions over there. The difference between the news of Nehemiah and that of the Christian family is that the Christian family's news is more glorious. They told him that the walls around Jerusalem were broken down and the gates had been burned and that the enemies from the outside were awaiting, laying the place to ruin.

But that is not the case and condition around the Christian Jerusalem. The walls around it is in good condition. They will never be torn down, for they were built by the Lord himself. They are built out of the best materials.

While on the isle of Patmos, St. John was allowed to take a look across the river and see the holy city, so he could send word to the Christian family, telling them the condition of the city and how the people are getting along over there.

He saw that the walls around the city were made of Jasper, and the streets were paved with gold. The gates were swung upon hinges of love, and there flowed around the city, a sea of everlasting love.

He also saw the people were happy and full of hope,

because the One who built the city is there, seated upon the throne. The four and twenty elders are bowed before Him crying, Holy. The majestic harpers are fluting music and the angels are flying from place to place. There is no night there on those shores, while the Saints from down below are waiting and watching for others to use their passport to come in.

Forever Being Guarded and Preserved by God
Text: Psalms 121:3-8

In this Psalm, we find Davidic Authorship. David's name is famous in Old Testament period for music and song and is closely associated with Holy Liturgy.

David was especially endowed by the Holy Spirit. Some call this Psalm the Soldier's Psalm, and they seem to think it was written in the camp when David was hazarding his life in the High Places of the Field, and trusted God to cover his head in the Day-Battle. Others call it the Traveler's Psalm, for there's nothing in it of military dangers, and it has been said that David designed it PRO VEHICULAR for the carriage, for a good man's convoy, and companion in a journey or voyage. But we need not thus appropriate it. Whenever we are at home or abroad, we are exposed to danger, more than we are aware of.

This Psalm directs and encourages us to repose ourselves and our confidence in house, and by faith, to put ourselves under His protection and commit ourselves to His care. This we must do with an entire resignation and satisfaction. In singing this Psalm, David here assures himself of help in verses 3-8, and all I have to do to get stirred up is read, *"He will not suffer thy foot to be moved,"* and in another Psalm He said, *"My feet had almost slipped, but the Lord stood by me."*

He will not suffer (in Hebrew: yaw-knack — meaning allow). He will not allow my foot to be moved. How do you know He won't Reverend? Just let me read the deed on the four corners of the Universe; *"The earth is the Lord's and the fullness thereof, the world, and they that dwell therein."*

Dr. Hammond, referring to Christ Incarnate, with whose humanity the deity being inseparably united, says God is always present with Him and through Him, with us for whom sitting at God's right hand, He constantly maketh intercession. He made Heaven and Earth, and He who could do that, can do anything. He made the world out of nothing, Himself alone, by a word, speaking in a little time and all was very good, very excellent, and beautiful.

Oh, yes, He can keep my foot from slipping. No matter how great our straits and difficulties, He has the power sufficient for our relief. He that made Heaven and Earth is Sovereign Lord of all, the Host of both and can make use of them as he pleases, for our help and restrain them when He pleases, from hurting His people.

1. Yes, He can speak to storms and they obey.
2. He can validate his word through a rooster.
3. He can tell a fish to swallow a prophet, take him to the bottom of the sea and wait on him to pray, then bring him to the shore and spit him out.
4. He can talk to Balaam through a donkey, who asked him, *"Why strike me these three times?"*

5. He can put highways in the middle of seas and rivers.

6. He can make an iron axe head float.

He's the Gheb-eer, meaning Master. He's Yaw, the Self-Existent One. He's Des-pot-ace, The absolute Ruler.

He's Kurios, Supreme Controller, He's Jehovah Jireh, the Lord will provide. He's Jehovah Rapha, the Lord that healeth, Jehovah Nissi, the lord our Banner. Jehovah Shalom, the lord our Peace. Jehovah Raah, the lord my Shepherd. Jehovah Tsidkenu, the lord our Righteousness. Jehovah Shammah, the lord is Present, this is my Protector.

He is thy Shade upon thy right hand. He not only protects those He keeps, but He refreshes them. He is Shade. The comparison has a great deal of Gracious Condescension in it. The Eternal Being who is Infinite Substance, is what He is, in order that He may speak sensible comfort to His people. He promises to be their Umbra, their Shadow, to keep as close to them and us, as the Shadow does to the body and to shelter them from the scorching heat, as the shadow of a Great Rock in a Weary Land.

He is always near to us, for our Protection and Refreshment, and never at a distance. He is our Keeper and Shade on the right hand. The sun shall not smite thee with his heat by day, nor the moon with her cold and moisture by night. He will keep us night and day, as He kept Israel in the wilderness — by a pillar of cloud by day (which screened them from the heat of the sun) and of a pillar of fire by night. The Lord shall preserve thee from all evil.

1. The evil of sin.
2. The evil of trouble.
3. And He will keep you from doing evil.

Whatever we suffer won't have any evil in it. Even that which kills us won't hurt us. He shall preserve thy soul. It's the Spiritual Life that God will take under his protection. He shall preserve—SODE-ZO—to save, protect or deliver.

YOUR SPIRITUAL LIFE
He's my Keeper
My Guard
My Deliverer
Oh, to be kept by JESUS;
Kept by the POWER OF GOD;
Kept UNSPOTTED FROM THE WORLD; treading where Jesus trod.
Oh, to be kept by JESUS,
Lord at thy feet I fall, I would be nothing, nothing, nothing
...Thou shalt be ALL-IN ALL.

Grasshopper Faith
Rev. Leon A. Brumfield,
Mount Horum Baptist Church, Fort Worth, TX

"And there we saw the giants, the sons of Anak, which come of the giants: and we were in our own sight as grasshoppers, and so we were in their sight." Numbers 13:30-33

Take note that Grasshopper Faith is not the size of a grasshopper. For the Word says, "If you have the faith of a mustard seed, then you can speak to the mountains" in your life and those mountains shall be removed. However, with Grasshopper Faith we are not making reference to the physical size but rather the spiritual size. I submit to you that Grasshopper Faith is so small spiritually, it is comparable to having no faith at all. With Grasshopper Faith, you cannot possess anything from the Lord. Grasshopper Faith focuses on what is seen physically.

The book of Hebrews tells us that "faith is the substance of things hoped for, the evidence of things not seen." So we see that faith operates in the unknown. It requires absolutely no faith to obtain what is already there. For the very definition of faith involves believing and not seeing. Grasshopper Faith thrives on what is already there. Since we cannot see our way through, Grasshopper Faith dictates to our spirit that it is not going to happen. Hebrews 11:6 states, "But without faith it is impossible to please God; for he that cometh to the Lord must believe that He is a rewarder of them that diligently seek him."

Here in the text, we see that Moses had sent out 12 spies to check out the Promised Land. Before the spies went, God had already told them that the land belonged to the Israelites. Each spy was a mirror image of the 12 tribes of the Israelites. Each spy agreed that the land was flowing with milk and honey. Yet, only 2 spies—Joshua and Caleb—trusted what God told them.

Now, we cannot be too hard on the spies, because many of us are like the 10 other spies. Preacher, what do you mean? How many times has God told us to do something and we do the exact opposite? The Word says, "Cast your cares upon Him for He careth for you."

God speaks to our spirit and tells us that job is ours, and we don't even fill out the application. God speaks to our spirit and tells us we are healed, and we have a setback which has us worrying and not trusting God. God speaks to our spirit and says what God has put together let no man put asunder. Yet, we have an argument with our spouse, and we are ready to throw in the towel. Or rather, God speaks to us and tells us, "I will bless you to pass this class." However, we fail the first exam and now considering dropping the course.

So, we all have doubted God at some point in our lives. Grasshopper Faith will keep us in the dark. Real faith requires us to trust God regardless of the situation. God tells us in His Word we are more than conquerors, but when the 'rubber hits the road' we shy away from our blessings. I really do believe that when we get to Heaven, we are going to see a stack of blessings we could have had if only we trusted God enough.

The 12 spies all had God's Word. The difference is what you do with His Word. God had already told them the land was theirs. God could have given them the land without any effort. However, God gave the Israelites the opportunity of obtaining the land by working for it.

As parents, we like to see our child or children put forth an effort first and then reward them with gifts. We take this kind of stance with our children, because we know when they work for something and receive it, they will appreciate that gift even more.

God treats us the same way we treat our children. God knows when we work for a common goal, we appreciate God's blessings even more.

If someone breaks a baby chick shell from the outside that chick would die. Yet, that chick has to struggle from the inside to see daylight. Struggles in life develop character. God gave the Israelites an opportunity to gain the Promised Land through battle. Instead of trusting God at His Word they saw giants over in the land and knew they could not possess the land. We need to look at how big is our God versus how big is our challenge. God allowed for that whole generation of Israelites to die out just because of their unbelief before entering the Promised Land. They wandered in the wilderness for forty years.

We know all about what God can do, yet we doubt Him. The Israelites saw how God delivered them from the Egyptians. The Israelites saw how God parted the Red Sea and blessed them to cross over on dry land. However, the 10 spies lost focus of the power of God. Grasshopper Faith feeds on negativity. God is steadily telling us "Yes" when we are saying "No." God says we can, but we are constantly saying we cannot.

Look at Romans 8:31. It says, "What shall we then say to these things? If God be for us who can be against us?" This verse is a direct challenge to our faith. What are we going to say to those things that trouble us? Are we going to view our strength in God, or are we going to view the strength in ourselves? I choose to trust in God, rather than myself. Jesus has already told us apart from him we can do nothing.

The 10 spies were looking at their feeble selves rather than trusting an almighty God. These 10 spies saw how God delivered them from the hands of Pharaoh and the Egyptians. We will always feel inadequate when we measure our own strength. Joshua and Caleb had Giant faith instead of Grasshopper faith. Joshua and Caleb trusted God for who He is. They had the faith that believed "God said it, and that settles it".

How many of us will take God for His Word? Philippians 4:13 illustrates, "I can do all things through Christ that strengthens me." As Christ as our source, we can accomplish the unbelievable. I knew when I went back to school to work on my MBA that this feat was going to be a serious challenge. After all, I had been out of school for 18 years. Yet, I trusted God that He would add the increase.

My counselor told me, "If you want something you never had you must do something you've never done."

I knew that God would bring me through. However, after three classes I had a major bipolar episode. I had to withdraw from school. Days looked pretty dark, but I knew God told me I would graduate with my MBA. A year after the episode, I enrolled back in school and completed my MBA in a year.

When our faith is challenged, we must respond rather than react. When we respond to the challenge, we find ourselves seeking God's guidance. Responding is much harder than just reacting, because our initial reaction is to act back naturally. While responding to our challenges find us responding spiritually.

This is evidence of the natural man versus the spiritual man. The natural man can only work with what he has, but the spiritual man has God as his resource. Don't you know the spiritual man has much more to draw from than the natural man? When we spiritually respond, we are trusting in God. Proverbs 3:5-6 states, "Trust in the Lord with all thine heart and lean not on thy own understanding. In all thy ways acknowledge him and he shall direct thy path." We have to trust and obey for there is no other way to be happy in Jesus but to trust and obey.

Trust is something that is earned and established. God earned our trust a long time ago. When God said, let there be light, and there was light. God earned our trust. Out of the entire Bible when God spoke, action was demanded or will come to pass. Unlike us, God has never gone against His Word. Even before King Hezekiah prayed, God knew He was going to grant him 15 more years of life.

God knew how his children, the Israelites, were treated in bondage to the Egyptians. God knew how he was going to deliver his children. God knows the pain and the anguish we as his children are experiencing. God has already made provision for us. God knew the pain we would experience having the Aids virus. God knew about the battle we would have with cancer. God knew and knows about our high blood pressure and heart trouble. God knows about our lack of faith. God is still telling us, "O ye of little faith." God knows about our Grasshopper Faith. God knows about the Giants we would face in our lives. God knows how fearful we would be staring at the Giants alone.

God allows some tragedies to happen to us to keep us humble. God could have killed all the Giants in the Promised Land before the children of Israel reached their destination. Yet, God let the spies see the Giants, because He knew His children would get the big head. God knows if we received everything we wanted when we expected, we like the Israelites would get beside ourselves. Sometimes, God has to filter out His children who have Grasshopper Faith. Grasshopper Faith will get you nowhere because these people are steadily comparing themselves to Giants.

Notice David, the Psalmist in Psalm 36:5, "Thy mercy, O Lord, is in the heavens; and thy faithfulness reacheth unto the clouds."

We need to have the type of faith to where we believe God's Word. God tells us we are the head and not the tail. God tells us we are more than conquerors. We today have all of God's Word from Genesis to Revelations from the beginning to the end. At this time in the text, the Israelites only had the books of the Law—Genesis, Exodus, Leviticus, Numbers and Deuteronomy.

We have a serious advantage over the Israelites because the Old Testament prophesied about Jesus years before Jesus came. Then, we see the power of Jesus Christ in the New Testament. How can a man feed 5,000 men not counting the women and children with two fish and five loaves of bread? This occurrence took more than Grasshopper Faith. Grasshopper Faith would have had one boy eating a fish sandwich and still be hungry!

We as God's children know what God can do. As believers, we can all say I know what God can do. In order to get anything from God requires us believing in God. We must believe that God is able. Just to know, God can do whatever needs to be done is special.

I am reminded of the three Hebrew boys who stood up for their God to King Nebuchadnezzar.

Shadrach, Meshach and Abednego said, "O king we will not bow down to you and let it be known our God is able to deliver us."

Just to know God is able demonstrates a real type of faith. This type of faith differs from Grasshopper Faith for two reasons. One is that real faith trusts in God. Secondly, real faith differs from Grasshopper Faith because real faith keeps the true and the living God in focus.

Keeping God in focus does not allow us time to focus on how big is our challenge or rather Giants. I know that my God is bigger than any challenge I will ever face. How do I know my God is bigger than any Giant? I know because He woke me up this morning and started me on my way. God has put food on my table. God has given me a reasonable portion of health and strength. God has never left or forsaken me. I have gone through different trials and tribulations, but God has been right there. Don't you know we serve a true and living God?

God has taken a little boy who would have to go to the hospital two to three times a week because of asthma. God has taken a young man who was diagnosed with a sugar level of 1500 and lived through it. God has taken a man who has had several bouts with bipolar disorder. God has taken a man who was unemployed and has blessed me to stay on the same job for 19 years.

I tell you I know what God can do. I know my redeemer lives. He lives in my heart. I have been through too much to have Grasshopper Faith. Grasshopper Faith is not for me or you. I am reminded of this song - Strong deliverer, strong deliverer be thou still my strength and shield. Bread of heaven, bread of heaven feed me till I want no more.

In A Nutshell
By Rev. J. Wilford Russell
First Timothy Baptist Church

"TRUST GOD'S LEADING"
Lesson: Numbers 13:25-28; 30-31; 14:6-10; 28-30
Golden Text: "If the Lord delight in us, then He will bring us into this land, and give it us; a land which floweth with milk and honey. Only rebel not yet against the Lord." (Numbers 14:8-9)

(A) Introduction:
    This week's lesson is based around the "discouraging report of the spies and the refusal of Israel to enter into Canaan." It will show that unbelief and disobedience can dishearten and defeat even the people of God. We will also see that God deals with rebellion in a forthright, decisive manner and that all who claim to be His must trust and obey.

(B) A decision made without seeking God's approval will result in failure.
    From Israel's encampment in the wilderness of Paran, Moses sent twelve chieftains (representing all the tribes except Levi) to search out the land of Canaan. This was permitted by God at the request of the Israelites who said: "Do let us send men ahead of us that they may

search out the land for us and bring us back word concerning the way by which we should go up and the cities to which we will come." (Deuteronomy 1:22-23).

Upon returning, all agreed that the land was indeed "flowing with milk and honey," but ten of the spies gave a faithless report that put fear into the Israelites. Only Joshua and Caleb encouraged them to go on into the land and take it. For Israel's lack of faith in listening to the bad report, God decreed that all the men who were twenty years of age and above should die in the wilderness during an extended period of forty years wandering. Joshua and Caleb were exceptions, and the tribe of Levi was not included.

(Numbers 13:1-33; 14:6-38; Deuteronomy 1:24-40)

(C) Standing firm against opposition (Numbers 14:6-10)

In these verses, we need to remember important truths about God. (1) God will do what pleases Him, and (2) What pleases Him will be good for them who belong to Him.

Caleb and Joshua, believing these truths, tried to encourage the rest of the people. There was one restriction noted by Caleb and Joshua. Joshua pleaded with the people not to "rebel" against God. To rebel means to believe that one's ideas are better and more important than God's, and, therefore, to be unwilling to submit to God. For the Israelites to rebel meant to refuse to enter the Promised Land. All believers need to remember that God honors faith and rewards obedience in all ages.

(D) The results of not trusting God (Numbers 14:28-30)

Disobedience and unbelief invite God's discipline. Persistent grumblings are also a petition to God to discipline your life. When you insist, God will give you your way—to your own regret.

(E) Summary

1. Children need to learn early that God's way is always the best way.

2. Fear can be a good thing because it often keeps us from danger.

3. Fear can also be paralyzing and can easily spread to other people.

4. God brings His people to critical decisions in their spiritual journey that provide special opportunities to show their trust in God.

5. God showers His blessings on those who trust and obey Him, but those who are filled with unbelief and refuse to obey Him will experience His extreme displeasure.

II. *IN A NUTSHELL*

PART 2: *"Love the Lord Your God"*

Lesson: Deuteronomy 6:1-13

Golden Text: "Hear, O Israel: The Lord our God is one Lord: and thou shall love the Lord thy God with all thine heart, and with all thy soul, and with all thy might." (Deuteronomy 6:4-5)

(A) Introduction:

A dictionary definition of love is: A feeling of warm

personal attachment or deep affection, as for a friend, for a parent, or child and so forth; also, the benevolent affection of God for His creatures or the reverent affection due from them to God; also, one of the synonyms for love is "devotion."

(B) Love highlighted

Love, kindness and consideration are well highlighted in Deuteronomy. The "LOVE" itself occurs twice as often in Deuteronomy as in Exodus, Leviticus and Numbers combined. Here we have the greatest commandment, (to which Jesus referred to in Matthew 22:36-37), uniquely stated — you must love the Lord your God with all your heart and all your soul and all your vital force (vs. 5).

God repeatedly expresses His love for Israel. The very tone of Deuteronomy highlights God's love for His people in chapter 5:29; "If only they would develop this heart of theirs to fear me and to keep all my commandments always, in order that it might go well with them and their sons to time indefinite.

(C) Knowledge of God and His purpose gives love right direction

Love must be first to God, above all others. Knowing God's purpose is essential and because one knows then what is best for his own welfare and that of others and will know how to express love in the proper way. This love to God is described in the Bible as loving Him with one's whole heart, mind, soul and strength. Love is primarily a quality of the heart. But if the mind is not equipped with knowledge of what true love is and how it acts, the heart's love can be expressed in the wrong direction.

In harmony with this, and since love is the most important quality, dedication to God is to the "person of the Lord" himself and is not to a work or a cause. Therefore, the soul, every fiber of one's organism, must carry out the love that is motivated by the heart and directed by the mind, and all one's strength must be put behind that effort.

(D) Concluding the Lesson

1. A holy fear of God is vital to the spiritual welfare of His children (Deut. 6:1-3).

2. It is impossible for one to please God without loving Him (Deut. 6:4-5).

3. Families who are pleasing to God are families who are rooted and grounded in His Word (Deut. 6:6-7).

4. Because there is no substitute for God's Word, it should have a prominent place in our lives and homes (Deut. 6:8-9).

5. Even though we do not (in any way) merit the grace of God, we enjoy it (Deut. 6:10-11).

6. Because of God's blessings, praise and thanksgiving should be in the heart and on the lips of every Christian (Deut. 6:12-13).

(E) Key Thought from the Lesson

Deut. 6:6-7 is just as relevant today as it was in

ancient Israel. God wants us not only to love him exclusively but also think about His commandments regularly. He wants us to teach His Word to our children and conform our daily lives to what the Bible says.

"IN A NUTSHELL"

Keep Moving—There is No Place to Park!
By Dr. C.W. Fields, B.A., D. D.

In the world today, in which we live, there's a definite parking problem. I hate to go downtown because the problem of the parking problem is so bad. I've noticed, while downtown, that there are temporary parking spaces; there are spaces where parking is absolutely forbidden; there are spaces that are assigned to certain people with their names written in these spaces. Even they can only park there during working hours.

There are parking meters where you may pay, and two hours is the limit on these, after which time you have got to move. Almost everywhere you look, there are No Parking Zones, and if you park there, it won't be long before a man or woman shows up, wearing a blue suit and a badge, and carrying a gun and a billy club. If they tell you to move on because there is no parking there, you either have to move on, or suffer the consequences.

The consequences are tickets, fines, or some other means of punishment. Sometimes they may even lock you up for parking in the wrong space or in a space where you are not wanted.

Now, let me say this, whenever God's people park in

this world, there is a NO PARKING ZONE. Christians have to keep on moving. This world has no parking spaces for God's people. The devil's people have all the Parking Spaces taken up, and anywhere a Christian parks, it's against Satan's law for him to park there. You see, when you park in Satan's territory, Satan gives you his laws, his rules, and his regulations.

Now, you have to watch Satan. He's a genius at disguising himself. He'll make it look like his way is right, but if you have some inside information, you won't park in his territory.

You see, every child of God ought to have some inside information. Every now and then, Jesus would take the disciples up into the mountain, or some desolate place and give them some inside information. God's people have been given some inside information. Because you just have to have it.

You know Satan attacked Jesus, and he's not going to pass you and me up. You have to be like Jesus to be saved—you can't just act like Jesus and be saved. But Satan will tell you that you can just act like Jesus and you can be saved. He knows how to attack, if he can't get the messenger, he'll just attack the message. If he can't get the servant, he'll attack the service. He wants us to accept the temporary and miss the eternal. You see, everything Satan has is just TEMPORARY, and only what you do for CHRIST will last.

Satan doesn't use the word "KINGDOM." He puts an "S" on his kingdom, making it plural, and the plurality means that there's something wrong with it. God has said, "The kingdoms of this world have become the Kingdom of our Lord and of His Christ, and He shall reign forever."

Satan wants to keep our minds little. He knows that if we can see HIGH things, we can reject LOW things. So, you have to watch Satan, and stay away from his parking meters. It'll cost you when you park in his zone—he fines us, locks us up, and gives us tickets. And in so many ways, some of our fines are to be flat on our backs, in a hospital, with some malignant disease, car wrecks, separations, divorces.

Standing in the Safety Zone

Text: "I know that my Redeemer liveth." Ps. 23, Job 19:25

In most of our great urban centers where the traffic is dangerous to pedestrians, especially in crossing the streets, one can find isles of safety, or safety zones, located out in the streets. From these safety zones, one can catch a bus, a trolley car, stop and rest awhile, or he can wait until the traffic passes by so that he can cross over safely. The very name itself, safety zone, is indicative of what it really is.

As long as an individual is in that safety zone he is pretty safe. In great cities, it is the business of the street police to see to it that pedestrians reach the safety zone. So it is in the church. The church is God's safety zone in this world, and it is the business of the gospel minister to see to it that men come into it because it is the only place which God guarantees as being safe. In the church, God Himself, with His almighty power, protects all who believe on Him.

Job of old was shaken by a many a wind and rolled by many a billow, but he was standing in God's safety zone. Any man who knows that God lives and predicates his life on such a belief is standing in God's safety zone. Paul said a child of God would be troubled on every side, but he would not be distressed; that he would be perplexed but not in despair; that he be persecuted, but he wouldn't be forsaken; that he would be cast down, but not destroyed. Paul assured us that when our load gets too heavy, God steps in to help us. (II Cor. 4:8-9)

In reviewing the life of Job, one wonders how he stood it all, but I Cor. 10:13 tells us that "God is faithful, who will not suffer you to be tempted above that ye are able; but will with the temptation also make a way of escape, that ye may be able to bear it."

God never leaves us alone. His eternal watch-care protects us all the way. If we are thirsty, he is a fountain of living water. He is a shadow from the heat. He is a refuge from your enemies. He is a fortress and a battle-axe in war. God never leaves us alone.

God did not leave Job. Job lost all his wealth. He was rich and became a pauper, but amidst all of his misfortune, God did not leave him.

God is a mighty good prop when you are about to fall. He is a mighty good leaning post, when you are about to go down. God promised to stay with us all the way. He promised to be with us in six troubles; and not to forsake us in the seventh. (Job 5:19)

God will not forsake His own, and He will answer if we call him. After a man has lost everything, he can still fall back on God. After Job lost all of his property, all ten of his children were killed in a cyclone. Job could not have withstood it if he had not been standing in the safety zone. God was Job's refuge and strength; his very present help in trouble. As Job stood in the presence of the bodies of his ten dead children, and as the tears rolled down his cheeks, he was heard to say, "The Lord giveth and the Lord taketh away. Blessed be the name of the Lord." (Job 1:21)

After Job lost all of his possessions and after all of his children died, then all of his earthly friends forsook him. But thank God, he was still standing in the safety zone. He remembered, no doubt, as he stood there without a friend in this world that, "...there is a Friend that sticketh closer than a brother, for He hath said, "I will never leave thee, nor forsake thee." (Prov. 18:24 and Heb. 13:5)

After Job lost his property, his children and his friends, he lost his health. Now he is broke, childless, friendless and sick, but he still keeps standing in the safety zone.

If you are a child of God, nothing can separate you from his love. Men did everything to Paul. He was in stripes above measure, in prisons frequently, and near death often. He said, "Of the Jews five times I received forty stripes save one. Thrice was I beaten with rods; once was I stoned; thrice I suffered shipwreck, a night and a day have I been in the deep; in journeyings often, in perils of mine own countrymen, in perils by the heathen, in perils in the city, in perils in the wilderness, in perils in the sea, in perils among false brethren; in weariness and painfulness, in watchings often, hunger and thirst; in fast--often, in cold and nakedness." (II Cor. 11:24-27)

Through it all we hear Paul saying, "Who shall separate us from the love of Christ? Shall tribulation, or distress, or persecution, or famine, or nakedness, or peril or sword? Nay, in all these things we are more than conquerors through Him that loved us. For I am persuaded that neither death, nor life, nor angels, nor principalities, nor powers, nor things present, nor things to come, nor height, nor depth, nor any other creature, shall be able to separate us from the love of God which is in Christ Jesus our Lord." (Rom. 8:35-39)

If you are a child of God nothing can separate you from His love.

If you are a child of God and if you are standing in the safety zone, you may get dead broke like Job, but God can give you some more money. You may get childless, but He can give you more children. You may lose your friends, but God can give you some more. You may get sick but God can get you well.

If you are a child of God – if you have been changed from nature to Grace – if your dungeon has been shaken and the chains of sin have fallen off – if the fallow ground of your heart has been broken up – if the Lord has spoken peace unto your soul – if you can say with Job, "I know that my Redeemer liveth," – if you know for yourself that you are standing in the safety zone, let come what may, God will take care of you.

You may be thrown into a lion's den like Daniel, but God can get you out. You may be cast into a fiery furnace, but God will take care of you. You may be arrested and thrown in jail like Paul and Silas, like Joseph and John Bunyan and a host of others. But if you are a child of God you'll come out all right.

God is all in all. God is too many things for us to fail. To the sick, He's the Great Physician. To the servant, He's the Good Master. To the lost, He's the Way. To the weary, He's the Giver of Rest. To the hungry, He's the Bread of Life.

God is all in all. He's too many things for a Christian to fail. He's the True Vine—He's the righteous judge—He's the Light of the World—He's the Everlasting Father—He's a Sure Foundation—He's the Lamb of God that taketh away the sins of the world. God is all in all. He is almighty. He is all powerful. He is all knowing. He is everywhere. He is all in all, and a child of God cannot fail.

Job couldn't fail. God is too many things for us to fail. He is above us. He's under us. He's with us, and we can't fail.

Don't be afraid of life. Don't be afraid of the journey if you are a child of God. Don't be afraid.

Favor and Leadership—an Overview
Reverend Damon L. Blakeley
Pastor, St. James African Methodist Episcopal Church Fort Worth, Texas

Let not mercy and truth forsake you; Bind them around your neck, Write them on the tablet of your heart, and so find favor and high esteem in the sight of God and man. (Proverbs 3:3-4, NKJV)

Leadership in the church may use insights from the secular world, but it is rooted in the faith "once delivered to the saints." Church leaders are first and foremost inspired by the Lord of the church, by the prophets and apostles, and by the fact that leadership is a gift, a calling, and a ministry.

A Gift. The New Testament is clear in stating that the church is a gifted community. It owes its very existence to a gift—the gospel of Jesus Christ. Its faith, its hope, its love, and the promises by which it lives are also seen as gifts. (1 Cor. 12:4-11)

However, while God's gifts to the church are many and varied, they are given for the common good, for the sake of the life, well-being, and mission of the church. Another way of saying it would be to say that God hereby appointed leaders for the church—leaders functioning in different capacities and in order to evoke and direct the gifts of others for the well-being of the church and its mission.

A Calling. The concept of the call is important. In the Old Testament, God called people into a covenant relationship, the basis of which is stated as follows: *"It was not because you were more in number than any other people that the Lord set His love upon you and chose you, for you were the fewest of all peoples; but it is because the Lord loves you..."* (Deut. 7:7,8a).

Our position in Christ is further stated by Peter in his first epistle, *"But you are a chosen race, a royal priesthood, a holy nation, God's own people, that you may declare the wonderful deeds of him who called you out of darkness."*

The call to leadership is, first, a call to a position. Second, the call to leadership is to a relationship, with both other leaders and the people to be led. Third, the call to leadership is a call to action. The apostles, prophets, and teachers of the early church were called not into honorary positions but to positions of action, with responsibilities to fulfill.

A Ministry. We know more clearly than in the past that ministry belongs to the whole people of God. We know, too, that ministry is service given in the name of Christ on behalf of or for the well-being of the church and its mission. Leadership as ministry is not only preparation for ministry, it is ministry when:

1. It guides the people of God, helping them fulfill their calling and mission.

2. It organizes the church so that maximum use is made of its resources.

3. It motivates people to affirm and participate in the life of the church.

In the words of Henri Nouwen, "Christian leadership is called ministry precisely to express that in the service of others new life can be brought about."

How do we become better leaders? Better yet, how do we grow as leaders of God's church to be effective in fulfilling the mission and purpose of the church?

CONDITIONS TO MEET

The Bible suggests to us that title does not necessarily include. God wants us to grow in _____, (fill in the blank). Obtaining spiritual wisdom isn't a one-a-week hobby. It is the daily discipline of a lifetime. But in this age of microwave ovens, fast foods, digests, and numerous "made easy" books, many people are out of the habit of daily investing time and energy in digging deep into Scripture and pursuing wisdom from the Lord.

Thanks to television, their attention span is brief. Thanks to religious entertainment that passes for worship, their spiritual appetite is feeble and spiritual knowledge isn't "pleasant to [their] soul" (Prov. 2:10). It's no wonder fewer and fewer people "take time to be holy" and more and more people fall prey to the enemies that lurk along the way.

"Your word I have hidden in my heart, that I might not sin against You." (Ps. 119:11, NKJV)

People are willing to work diligently in their jobs because they know they'll earn a paycheck. But what about applying themselves diligently to God's Word in order to gain spiritual riches that are more valuable than gold and silver and jewels—riches that will last forever? (See 2:4, 3:13-15; 8:10-21; 16:16)

There's a price to pay if we would gain spiritual wisdom, but there's an even greater price to pay if we don't gain it. We must walk with God through the study of His Word.

We are separated people—in dress, in conduct, in conversation, in loyalty, in gratitude, in firmness and in spirituality. This America boasts of being the "land of the free and the home of the brave."

First of all, we are not free---it is dangerous to walk the street, or even remain at home. I do not refer to the intimidation we meet with other races but we are against one another.

The Church is not suffering because of the action of Birmingham, Selma, Montgomery nor Mississippi, yet that is a part of it. Think of the suffering, the wars, the head on collisions, the airplane crashes. This is a disgraced world and sin is the cause of it all. There are those persons on board the ship who should listen to the advice of the man with the keys in his hands. Paul was prisoner on board, but he had the keys, he told the ship officers not to set sail, for the voyage would only bring danger and frustration. He knew what he was talking about, for there stood by him that night, an angel of God whose he was. Biblical records will show that God has sustained the prophets in all ages. He is God's Key Man.

Enoch walked on by the moon and speaking in a common term, he threw love kisses at the stars and played "tic-tac" with the sun. Elijah was escorted with courtesy of God sending the sun in the form of a chariot.

Paul makes it very beautiful. "We are troubled on every side yet not in distress, perplexed but not in despair, persecuted but not destroyed, for we that are in this tabernacle do groan."

All of this approving ourselves ministers of God, in patience, afflictions, necessities, in distresses, in stripes, in imprisonment, in tumult and in labor.

By pureness, by knowledge, by longsuffering, by kindness, by the Holy Ghost, by love unfeigned. By honor and dishonor—as unknown and yet well known. As poor yet making many rich. In other words, I hold a very unique position in the set of the Kingdom of God. I can unlock and tap the resources of God. Break up prisons, call fire out of Heaven, walk on water and fill the widow's meal barrel.

This is a disturbed social order. We have never had so many fine houses and such few homes, we have never had so many elaborate schools and yet so many dropouts. We have never had so many hospitals and yet so many with no beds available. We have never had so many deacons, yet we run to courts with much of our church affairs. We have never had so many ushers and yet very little peace and order in the church.

Scientifically, the world is supposed to be round, radically it is one sided. Mathematically, it is divided. Domestically, it is crooked. Educationally, it is top heavy. Geometrically, it is out of reach. Biologically, it is beyond reasoning. Athletically, it is in a hurry. Musically, it is out of tune. Spiritually it is cold and flat. But you are God's Key Man and you are equal to the situation.

God's minister holds a very unique position. You are a minister, not a mystical misfit. You are a preacher, not just a public speaker. You are chosen of God not a choice of yours. You are elected of God, not of the crowd. Your authority is from Heaven, not Washington. You are not a fisherman by trade, but must catch men. You are not a philanthropist, but you must endow and assure some fallen man of eternal life. You are not a banker, but you must give specification and plans for the construction of God's church. You are not a doctor but you must lay hands on the sick. You are not the captain of the Salvation Army, but thousands of underprivileged must be clothed by your command.

What is the Anointing of the Holy Spirit?
Sermon By Rev. Timothy J. Winters
Pastor, Bayview Baptist Church

In recent years, the ministry of the Holy Spirit has been receiving more attention than at any time in the history of the Church, and at times the Holy Spirit is recognized to the exclusion of the ministry and work of Jesus Christ!

In many instances, the ministry of the Holy Spirit is being grossly exaggerated. Actually, it is more correct to say that in some instances the ministry of the Holy Spirit is being DISTORTED! An Unbiblical viewpoint of the ministry of the Holy Spirit is being espoused on a large scale to an unsuspecting audience. This exaggerated viewpoint of the ministry of the Holy Spirit comes out of a Christian circle that is identified as the **Faith Movement**. Ministers in the *"faith movement"* take extreme personal liberties in interpreting the Scriptures. They violate the warning given in 2 Peter 1:20 that says, *"no prophecy of scripture is of private interpretation."*

Some of the more prominent ministers of the *"faith movement"* have popularized the prevalent emphasis of the anointing of the Holy Spirit, commonly called *"The Anointing."* The anointing of the Holy Spirit, by their interpretation, is taught in connection with a phenomenon (which is not a phenomenon) called, "*slain in the Spirit.*" The experience of being "*slain in the Spirit*" has no biblical basis at all! And their interpretation of the anointing of the Spirit does not have any biblical basis either.

The first thing necessary is to get a clear understanding of the ministry of the Holy Spirit in a general sense. The overall ministry of the Holy Spirit was different in Old Testament times than in New Testament times. When we observe the ministry of the Holy Spirit in the Old Testament times, the ministry of the Holy Spirit was primarily EXTERNAL.

In New Testament times, His ministry is primarily INTERNAL. In Old Testament times, His ministry was primarily TEMPORARY. In New Testament times, His ministry is PERMANENT. In the days of the Old Testament, He would come UPON people for a specific ministry for a specific time. Example: David prayed for the Lord not to take the Holy Spirit from him (Ps. 51:11). No Christian ever needs to pray that prayer! The Holy Spirit's ministry was transitory in David's time. The ministry and movement of the Holy Spirit was periodic in Old Testament days.

Specifically, concerning the anointing of the Holy Spirit, we must also first consider the general meaning of anointing. In the rules of Biblical Interpretation, there is the rule called the Law of First Mention. The way to get to the essence of the meaning of an act, procedure, or a word is to observe its first appearance in Scripture. The word, "anoint," appears for the first time in Exodus 28:14.

> *"And you shall put them upon Aaron, your brother, and his sons with him; and shall anoint them, and consecrate them, and sanctify them that they may minister unto me in the priest's office."*

This text is the record of God instructing Moses in initiating the priesthood through Aaron and his sons. Exodus 28:40 is a description of the priestly garments that they were to wear. So, verse 41 begins by saying, "You shall put them (the priestly garments) upon Aaron and his sons…" Then it mentions specifically, "…and shall anoint them, and consecrate them, and sanctify them…" The basic meaning of anointing is to externally douse, pour, or drench a person or an object. It was also done by rubbing or massaging salve or ointment. The common liquid for anointing was oil. Oil is one of the main symbols of the Holy Spirit! In the case mentioned in Exodus 28:41, the anointing of Aaron and his sons was accomplished by pouring oil upon them.

God said to "anoint them and consecrate (Heb. male: fill, accomplish, prepare) them." "…and sanctify (quadash: dedicate, hallow, separate) them." The basic meaning of sanctify is to set aside for service unto God.

From Exodus 28:41 we have the first mention of "anoint" and get the first meaning which is twofold: to consecrate (prepare) and sanctify (set apart) for the priest's office. The anointing was symbolically done by pouring oil upon Aaron and his sons.

In the New Testament, the first time "anoint" is used in connection with service unto God, is in Luke 4:18:

> *"The Spirit of the Lord is upon me, because He has anointed me to preach the gospel to the poor; He has sent me to heal the brokenhearted, to preach deliverance to the captives and recovering of sight to the blind, to set at liberty them that are bruised."*

Matthew 6:17 has a reference to "anoint." This was when Jesus taught that people should anoint themselves and wash themselves when fasting. Mark 16:1 has a reference to "anoint." This was the occasion when the women were coming to the tomb to complete the burial process for the body of Jesus. Luke 7:46 has a reference to "anoint." This was when Jesus rebuked Simon, His dinner host, for not properly addressing Him upon His arrival to his house and for not having refreshing water available and scented oil for His hair.

However, the first reference to "anoint" for service unto God is Luke 4:18. Note the reading of the text, it says, "The Spirit of the Lord is U-P-O-N me…" Being upon or coming upon a person was the Old Testament ministry of the Holy Spirit. We must realize that Jesus was subject to, and lived in submission to, the Old Testament Dispensation of the ministry of the Holy Spirit.

Gal. 4:4 says, "…God sent forth His Son, made of a woman, made under the law…" Jesus lived, ministered, and died under the Old Testament Dispensation of the Law. So, the ministry of the Holy Spirit in Jesus' time was the same as it was in Old Testament times. That's why the text says "The Spirit of the Lord is U-P-O-N me…" The Holy Spirit performed an external ministry at that time. (The New Testament Dispensation did not occur until the Day of Pentecost was fully come.) Jesus was anointed to begin His ministry of redemption. Meaning that He was consecrate and sanctified for that purpose. There are two other references to the anointing of Jesus: Acts 4:27, 10:38.

Aside from the references to Jesus being anointed for service, there are only three other references of anointing by the Holy Spirit that relate to believers in general. Those scriptures are 2 Cor. 1:21; John 2:20, 27.

"Now He who establishes us with you in Christ, and has anointed us, is God." (2 Cor. 1:21)

"But you have anointing from the Holy One, and you know all things." (I John 2:20)

"But the anointing which you have received of Him abides in you, and you need not that any man teach you; but as the same anointing teaches you of all things, and is truth, and is no lie, and even as He has taught you, ye shall abide in Him." (I John 2:27)

All of the aforementioned Scriptures show that the anointing of the Holy Spirit is a present tense occurrence. It is not something that a person has to seek, pursue and finally achieve. It is commonly, but unbiblically taught that a person must maintain a high-level quality of life in order to "keep the anointing."

Also, a correct interpretation of those verses will show that the anointing of the Holy Spirit is not reserved for a select few, special, or spiritual Christians. The anointing of the Holy Spirit is not selective, it is collective. The application of the anointing of the Holy Spirit is meant for the entire Corinthian church. "You in Christ" is plural. Likewise, John's application of the anointing of the Holy Spirit was for the collective body of believers who would read his epistle.

Another troublesome matter with the misinterpretation of the anointing of the Holy Spirit, is that it is confused with the meaning of the filling of the Spirit. The anointing of the Holy Spirit is to consecrate (prepare) and to sanctify (set apart) for service to God.

Whatsoever!
Philippians 4:10-14

"Not that I speak in respect of want: for I have learned, in whatsoever state I am, Therewith to be content. I know both how to be abased, and I know how to abound: everywhere and in all things I am instructed both to be full and to be hungry, both to abound and to suffer need. I can do all things through Christ which strengthens me."

Here in the text, we find the Apostle Paul using the term "whatsoever." Here is a word that has gained much popularity in our community. We can find many people using this term. However, this terminology has been pinned as having a negative connotation. Young people are found using whatsoever in a negative sense. People often use this word to turn away others who might be bothering them. Whatsoever often implies to the sender as if one does not care. Today, I hope to broaden your scope of the word whatsoever.

The Apostle Paul uses this term whatsoever, however, in a positive sense. Paul, in other words, is saying no matter what comes my way I will be content. Here Paul implies that no matter what the issue or circumstance, he states he will be content. Paul, a seasoned veteran, says he will be content. It takes some suffering to get to this point in life. Whether Paul is up or whether he is down, Paul is determined to be content. One may say that they will be content, but unless a person has experienced being on both sides of the coin such a statement will not have much meaning. Only until a person has been up and down, he or she does not know how they will respond. God is using Paul as an instrument to God's people. Paul had been in prison several times, only guilty of spreading God's word.

Hear Paul in 2 Corinthians 11:24-27 as he says, *"Of the Jews five times received I forty stripes save one. Thrice was I beaten with rods, once was I stoned, thrice I suffered shipwreck, a night and a day I have been in the deep; In journeying often, in perils of waters, in perils of robbers, in perils by mine own countrymen, in perils by the heathen, in perils in the city, in perils in the wilderness, in perils in the sea, in perils among false brethren; In weariness and painfulness, in watching often, in hunger and thirst, in fasting often, in cold and nakedness."*

Paul has truly suffered for God in many ways. Yet, Paul knew that if we suffer with God, we will reign with Him. Isn't it a sad case when a person suffers with no cause? Paul says in 2 Timothy 2:12, "If we suffer, we shall also reign with him; if we deny him, he also will deny us." It is indeed an honor and a blessing to suffer for the cause of Christ.

Verse 11 of the text reads, "Not that I speak in respect of want: for I have learned, in whatsoever state I am, therewith to be content."

To break down this verse, Paul is stating, "Not that I am implying that I was in any personal want, for I have learned how to be content (satisfied to the point where I am not disturbed or disquieted) in whatever state I am."

Here this letter finds Paul in a condition of contentment. Regardless, what comes his way Paul has learned to be content. My dad had preached a sermon called "Lessons to Learn" before he passed away. Now, I know the true meaning of that message. We all have lessons to learn in this life. However, when we can learn to be content in whatsoever state is the most vital lesson we can learn. Not that Paul stopped learning in this life, but he learned to be content.

Some of us as believers pray the most selfish prayers. Lord give me a 3200 square feet home. Lord give me a Cadillac so I can ride in style. Lord give me a new career. Lord give me my healing. Lord give me this and give me that. We treat God as some kind of glorified sugar daddy. In the words of Janet Jackson we say what have you done for me lately?

There is nothing wrong with asking God for what we want or need. Yet, there should be times we need to pray what will you have me to do Lord? Or rather, not my will but thine will be done. When we can shift the focus from what we want to what God wants us to do, then we will find peace and be blessed. This sign represents a mature Christian.

God tells us that He knows what we need. God will continue to give us what we need, but He wants us to put Him first. Matthew 6:33 says, "But, seek ye first the kingdom of God and his righteousness; and all these things shall be added unto you."

God knows what we need and knows how to bless us. Can't nobody do me like Jesus. When we put God first, God has a way of putting our wants and needs first. That is why Paul can say "whatsoever state I am in." Paul had learned some key lessons throughout his walk with God. Paul had come to know God in a personal way. Paul knew God would provide for him because Paul had seen God's provisions actively working in his life.

Paul's faith had been put to test in several ways. Paul knew that if it was God's will, he would make it through whatsoever he was facing. Paul said, "I have learned to be content." Paul had seen God's mighty hand at work on several occasions. Paul knew that he can have peace in the midst of a storm. Paul walked in confidence knowing that God is able. Don't you know that God can bring you through whatsoever you are facing?

Don't you know God can bring you through Aids? Don't you know God can bring you through heart trouble? Don't you know God can bring you through cancer? Don't you know God can bring you through unemployment? Don't you know God can bring you through marital issues? Don't you know God can bring you through whatever you may be facing? God does not put more on us than we can bear. When we are going through the storms of life, it is a testimony of how strong we are in the Lord. Earth has no problems that Heaven cannot heal.

Have you ever been in a situation where you saw no

way out? I have been in several situations where I saw no way out. One time, I had too much to drink and ran out of a friend's house to jump in my car. I drove five miles at night with no lights on. I ended up crashing my car slightly on my parents' garage. God spared me that night only to warn me about leaving the Lord out of your plans. Someone is already planning a wedding, and you have not asked God for a mate. I hear Paul on another occasion saying "be ye also ready." Paul went on to say that the Lord will come as a thief in the night.

One person may say, "I know that God exists, but I will accept him when I get older." Funeral homes are designing small caskets just like big caskets. When we even have brutality within our Police system, the time is now to draw closer to the Lord. When innocent African-American men are getting murdered by the police, it is time to draw closer to the Lord. The Lord says "draw nigh unto me and I will draw nigh unto you."

You better recognize we are living in the last days. As soldiers of the cross, we must be on our mission of witnessing for the Lord. Just let your friend know how good God has been to you. God has been good to all of us. He woke me up this morning and started me on my way. He put food on my table. God gave me a reasonable portion of health and strength. He gave me the activities of my limbs. Don't you know God is good—all the time? And all the time—God is good!

This fact is reason enough for us to proclaim that regardless of the circumstance, I will trust in the Lord. I will trust in the Lord until I die. We too can also say like

Paul—whatsoever state I am in, I will be content.

I remember Job's confession. Though He slay me, yet will I trust Him. Job was determined not to let anything deter him from trusting God. Job, like Paul, knew that all things work together for good to them that love God, and to them that are called according to His purpose. Some things that happen to us may not be good. However, we know that God will work it out for the good. It is just like lemonade. Lemons are sour, but when you make lemonade the drink is sweet. God takes our lemons that happen to us in life and sweetens them to lemonade.

We serve an all-caring type of God. God cares for you and me. Since we have established that God cares for us, and we know we can depend on God. God is omniscient. God is omnipresent, and God is omnipotent. God knows everything. God is everywhere at the same time. God also has all power in his hands. Who would not want a God like this God on his or her side? Paul knew that being in the will of God had its privileges. Paul knew he could be content in God, because God is in total control. Do we have that same level of trust in God? Since we know God is able, we too, like the Hebrew boys, can be content.

Just to know that God is able is reason enough to serve Him. The Hebrew boys, Shadrach, Meshach, and Abednego, were convinced that serving the Lord pays off. These boys were facing the fiery furnace. They knew that not bowing down to king Nebuchadnezzar meant being thrown in the fire. However, they would rather be thrown in the fire than to dishonor their God. These boys made up their minds that they would rather be content in God than to serve man. They served God in spite of whatsoever consequences they had to face.

These young men were not the only ones who served God instead of man. Hebrews 11 lists an entire group who ignored the consequences to serve God. Hebrews 11:6 and following reads, "But without faith it is impossible to please him: for he that cometh to God must believe that he is, and that he is a rewarder of them that diligently seek him.

"By faith Abel offered unto God a more excellent sacrifice than Cain, by which he obtained witness that he was righteous. By faith Enoch was translated that he should not see death; and was not found, because God had translated him: for before his translation he had this testimony, that he pleased God. By faith Noah, being warned of God of things not seen as yet, moved with fear, prepared an ark to the saving of his house; by which he condemned the world, and became heir of the righteousness which is by faith.

"By faith Abraham, when he was called to go out into a place which he should after receive for an inheritance, obeyed; and he went out, not knowing whither he went. By faith he sojourned in the land of promise, as in a strange country, dwelling in tabernacles with Isaac and Jacob, the heirs with him of the same promise. By faith also Sara herself received strength to conceive seed, and was delivered of a child when she was past age, because she judged him faithful who had promised.

"By faith Abraham, when he was tried, offered up

Isaac: and he that had received the promises offered up his only begotten son. By faith Isaac blessed Jacob and Esau concerning things to come. By faith Jacob, when he was dying, blessed both the sons of Joseph; and worshipped, leaning upon the top of his staff. By faith Joseph, when he died, made mention of the departing of the children of Israel; and gave commandment concerning his bones.

"By faith Moses, when he was come to years, refused to be called the son of Pharaoh's daughter; choosing rather to suffer affliction with the people of God, than to enjoy the pleasures of sin for a season. By faith they passed through the Red sea as by dry land: which the Egyptians assaying to do were drowned. By faith the walls of Jericho fell down, after they were compassed about seven days. By faith the harlot Rahab perished not with them that believed not, when she had received the spies with peace."

By faith Dr. Martin Luther King, Jr. fought for equal rights through his non-violent movement. By faith Nelson Mandela became President of South Africa and brought about an end to Apartheid. By faith Pastor F. S. Moody, Sr. preached the word and grew Mount Horum from a small church to having a membership of over 500 people. By faith great people did great things.

We should not worry about the whatsoever states that come up in life. I know my God is able. I am going to be content like Paul. Lessons in life has matured me to the point of whether I am abased or abounding, I will trust God. The same God that saved me, He is the same

God that can keep me. The same God that can keep me, He is the same God that can lead me. The same God that can lead me, He is the same God that can protect me. Don't you know serving God pays off right now?

Philippians 4:6-8 says, "Be careful for nothing; but in everything by prayer and supplication with thanksgiving let your requests be made known unto God. And the peace of God, which passeth all understanding, shall keep your hearts and minds through Christ Jesus. Finally, brethren, whatsoever things are true, whatsoever things are honest, whatsoever things are just, whatsoever things are pure, whatsoever things are lovely, whatsoever things are of good report; if there be any virtue, and if there be any praise, think on these things. Those things, which ye have both learned, and received, and heard, and seen in me, do: and the God of peace shall be with you."

Jesus—He's my rock in a weary land. Jesus—He's my shelter in the time of a storm. Jesus—He's the lily of the valley. Jesus—He's my bright and morning star. Jesus—He's bread when I am hungry. Jesus—He's water when I am thirsty. Jesus—He's that wheel in the middle of a wheel. Jesus—He's a mother for the motherless. Jesus—He's a father for the fatherless. Jesus—He's a sister for the sisterless. Jesus—He's a brother for the brotherless. Jesus—He'll be a friend for the friendless.

Don't you know Jesus careth for you?

You can make it through the whatsoever's of life by submitting your life to Christ! That's why Paul concludes by saying I can do all things through Christ that strengthens me. You can make it through life. I don't care whether you are suffering from sickness. I don't care if you are pressured to join a gang. I don't care if you lost your job and don't know how the bills will get paid. You can make it if you try. You do not have to commit suicide. This whatsoever in your life will pass. James Cleveland said, "This too shall pass."

You can make it with the blood of Jesus. I dare you to plead the blood over your circumstance or problem. You see, they hung Him high and stretched Him wide, for you and for we He died. He died. Didn't He die? He stayed dead all night Friday. He stayed dead all night Saturday. But early Sunday morning, He got up with all power in his hands. I know my God is able for He lives in me. He walks with me, and He talks to me, He tells me I'm his own. Many people have counted me out, but God keeps on blessing me. Over and over.

> *What a fellowship? What a joy divine? Leaning on the everlasting arms. What a blessedness, what a peace is mine, leaning on the everlasting arms. Leaning, leaning, safe and secure from all alarms. Leaning, leaning, leaning on the everlasting arms.*
>
> *Oh, how sweet to walk in this pilgrim way, Leaning on the everlasting arms. Oh, how bright the path grows from day to day, leaning on the everlasting arms. What have I to dread, what have I to fear, leaning on the everlasting arms? I have blessed peace with my Lord so near, leaning on the everlasting arms.*

ZION'S WAKE UP CALL

What Can God Trust You With?
Sister Goldine Long

Trust: in the care and possession of a trustee; permit to stay or to go or to do: without fear or misgiving; rely on the truthfulness or accuracy of; extend credit to; assured reliance on the character, ability, strength or truth of someone. - Webster's Collegiate

Now that we know the definition of trust, we present the question again, "What can the Lord trust you with?" As I thought about Jesus Christ, and where He brought me from, I was actually able to see the place. It was utter darkness, just like He said in 1 Peter 2:9. It was a place where no light brightens your path and no joy comes in the morning. A place of despair, without hope and without God.

It appeared to be a place of wishful thinking, daydreams, misplaced trusts and disappointments. The population consisted of those who lived in "adultery, fornication, uncleanness, lasciviousness, idolatry, witchcraft, hatred, heresies, envying, murders, drunkenness, reveling, and such like…" (Gal. 5:19-21)

Then I saw myself (in the flesh & lacking salvation). I was cast down, rebuked, wounded and left for dead. A common denominator reduced to the lowest terms. A slave to evil—tested, tried, and found wanting. A liar, selfish, unconcerned, void of understanding, lacking wisdom, and knowledge of God.

I needed help, but, where could I turn? Who could I run to? I had no more solutions, I had tried everything twice, but I still had no love, no peace and no joy.

Life has a way of helping you come to yourself, doesn't it? Well, I came to myself and gave up my way. And something wonderful happened to me, I opened my eyes and there stood JESUS—the Way, the Truth, and the Life. He stood strong and courageous, pure and holy, loving and kind, tender and merciful. (Some people don't know to this day the meaning of such words.) He presented Himself as a Prophet and revealed to me the Word of God, as a Teacher. He taught me to accept the entire Word of God and apply it to my daily life, as a Guide, he led me out of that place of darkness. Bless His Name.

As I looked around the Kingdom of God, what I saw next is called "Amazing Grace." God had bought my liberty. He paid the price for my redemption. Today, I am free in Christ. I saw a Creator, who truly loves His own—so much so He devised an infallible plan for our lives. Now I can declare to you—our faith and trust in Jesus and obedience to His Word is absolutely necessary to sanction our salvation and our eternal abode with Him.

Yes there is place prepared for us, and Jesus is

coming again, but we are told to occupy until He comes. If we stumble in our daily walk and find that we have not reached our highest height or our deepest depth in Christ, and if we are on the wrong path with too great a distance between us and the Lord, we need to trust Him more.

The Lord needs Zion to Wake Up. There is a great harvest and workers are needed in the vineyard. Each of us has a vineyard. Some are smaller, and some are larger, some are nearer or further away than others. But are you working? Can Jesus depend on you to be faithful over a few things? Where are we laying up our treasurers? You know where your treasure is, there will your heart be. (Matthew 6:20)

Sure, we suffer many things when we are involved in relationship, but our ministry is one of reconciliation, and that involves dealing with people. Are you praying for friends, loved ones, and enemies, or are you a help or a hinder to God's program? But do you manage the love that God has shed abroad in your heart? Treat others as you want to be treated.

Yes, of course Jesus is Wonderful, Counselor, Mighty God, Everlasting Father, but He is looking for a friend — someone He can trust. You say you know Him. So answer this, if you will. "What Can The Lord Trust You With?"

Only you know the answer, only you know the truth.

Lads with his Mother's Blessings
By Rev. R. W. Collins

"There is a lad here, which hath five barley loaves, and two small fishes." John 6:9

This statement was made by one of the disciples while pondering the question of feeding the multitude one day in the wilderness. A great throng had followed Jesus to the country away from the business center to hear him preach and teach, and while out there, they got hungry.

They were being filled with spiritual food, but at the same time, the want of physical food seized upon them. One of the great driving forces of the human family is hunger. Man is always hungry for things and has always been able to answer hunger's quest somehow.

Knowing how far they were from the city, and finding how little money was in the treasury, they thought about a certain lad there in the midst who had a lunch. One which his mother had prepared for him before sending him away.

Great mothers are always thoughtful about their lads and lasses. They always prepare for them before sending them out to mix with the crowd, and too, there are always some grown-ups who know what lads and lasses have to offer.

There, Andrew, Simon Peter's brother, said to Jesus, "There is a lad here with five barley loaves and two small fishes. But what is that in a crowd like this?"

Jesus ordered them to "bring him to me."

This boy's lunch was a very valuable asset, because it was prepared by his mother, and carried to Jesus for an increase. His lunch was multiplied to the extent, that the whole crowd was blessed with it.

The lesson of the text is universal in scope and can be applied to boys and girls of all walks of life and all ages of the world. For each of them has something to offer.

However, it becomes the duty of the folk back home to wrap their lunches before sending them out to jostle with the crowd. If the package is well chosen, as to kind and content, the world will be pleased to use it. If the right things are wrapped at home, the world will be compelled to use them. For they will surely serve the purpose. Some mothers will send their children away from home without having done anything to secure their future.

Our streets are filled with boys and girls today who have been sent out to mingle with the crowd without having been given anything to go on. On the other hand, some have been given things to go on, but threw them down along the way. They didn't want to be bothered. The package was too cumbersome. It was too much trouble to drag along.

This word of warning to mothers who have boys and girls to be sent out to join this human throng of life seekers—be careful about the kind of lunch you prepare for their journey. Whatever you do, don't give them something that will spoil before time to use it. The mother of the text did not give her son tainted fish and stale bread. The food she gave him was fresh and well-prepared. It was her aim to see to it that her child was secure against the trials of the wilderness. She wanted him to be able to survive the pangs of hunger even though others starved.

But when she prepared for hers, she prepared for three thousand others. Life has fixed it so that in preparing for yourself, you prepare for thousands. Whenever you give your child the proper things to meet tomorrow's crisis, you are also helping to bless the world. For it matters not how small the lunch of life might be, more than one will be blessed by it.

The mother of the boy of the text was thinking about his physical needs, but the boys and girls of this age have greater needs. The packages which their mothers wrap for them must reach into every field, serve every need, and cover every purpose.

We know that every child should have a lunch when going out to work or play. Whatever they do, they should be well fed. But there are many things more valuable than eating food, and there are many things which mothers and fathers can wrap for their children before sending them out that will be more helpful to the world than the fish and bread, which was given by the mother to her son in the text.

The boys and girls of today must be given a well-prepared lunch of home training. They should be taught at home how to support themselves when they go out to mingle. Their educational lunch must be prepared if we expect them to sustain and endure the wilds of the wilderness life. One of the shortcomings of our time is we fill the children's educational lunch with trash, when the need is for hard, solid food. Is it any wonder the children of this generation are so light in mind? They have nothing but trash to feed on. Funny papers, comic books, novels and fiction are the things which go to make up the reading matter for the youngsters of our day. How can they make the mark in life?

We must wrap in their lunches honor and respect for the older people. To send a child out in life without teaching him to honor those who are older than he means a defeat before he starts. The boy of the text has a wonderful mother, for she had his interest at heart. She felt that it was her duty to look after the interest of her child, and not leave those responsibilities to others. They no doubt could do some minor things in helping him through, but it was her duty to do the major. Therefore, before sending him out, she wrapped his lunch.

Her boy became the center of attraction to both Jesus, and the multitude, because he had what Jesus could use in helping them. And too, the boy didn't misuse his lunch. He kept it in good condition until the right time. Then, if the mothers and fathers do the right thing for the boy and girls of this generation, they must wrap and give them a proper lunch before sending them out. Andrew said to Jesus, "There is a lad here with two small fishes and five loaves."

In every crowd can be found boys and girls with things of value that can be used to help others. Especially, if the people at home have been faithful in doing their part.

The Peace of God
SUBMITTED BY REV. JULIUS L. JACKSON JR., MACEDONIA MISSIONARY BAPTIST CHURCH, PASTOR/TEACHER

"Do not be anxious about anything, but in everything by prayer and supplication with thanksgiving let your requests be made known to God. And the peace of God, which surpasses all understanding, will guard your hearts and your minds in Christ Jesus." Philippians 4:6-7 (ESV)

Stress is the word that we use to describe the effects of anxiety or worry. The word "worry" is a synonym for anxiety, and it comes from an Old English word meaning "to choke or strangle." That is exactly what worry or anxiety does to our peace, productivity and joy.

Someone has observed that worry is the Christian's most popular sin because it is the one that we don't even try to disguise. Worry is so common in our lives that we are not even particularly ashamed of it. "Worry is the interest we pay on tomorrow's troubles." "Worry pulls tomorrow's cloud over today's sunshine." "Worry gives a small thing a big shadow." So as Bobby McFerrin reminds us, every life has trouble. Worry doubles that trouble. We aren't supposed to worry.

These are chaotic times. We live in a time where you have a president who used to chant "lock her up," who now appears to be headed to lock up. We live in a time where news is considered fake. North Korea tests missiles in order to have a photo opportunity with an egotistical president for its own propaganda purposes. Where Putin and Russia determine the outcome of our free and fair elections. We live in a time, where you have to take a knee to protest and draw attention to police brutality against blacks. We live in a time of no justice but just us. For the record, I'm not being political, I'm being prophetic. These are chaotic times. Chaotic is an adjective that comes from the noun "chaos," meaning complete and total confusion or lack of order. Many of us worry about the situation of the world. We don't know when the bombs will explode. We feel that we are living our secret storms on the edge of night while searching for tomorrow. The situation of our times is dangerous.

- Roads are not safe due to road rage and reckless driving.
- The family is fractured. Parents used to be in charge, but children are giving orders.
- Disconnection from meaningful relationships. People would rather text you than talk to you.
- Financial struggles. Too many bills. People living high begging for what they need.
- Hurricanes, tsunamis and other weather disasters leading to unprecedented death and destruction.
- Mentally deranged. Self-medicating trying to

feel better. The world is spinning so fast, until you want to say, stop world and let me off.

All of this leads to worry and anxiety. The noted author, Chuck Swindoll calls worry the "universal addiction." Paul understood the natural tendency to become anxious. He knew that anxiety is one of the greatest thieves of joy. So he writes (according to the Amplified Bible): *"Do not be anxious or worried about anything, but in everything [every circumstance and situation] by prayer and petition with thanksgiving, continue to make your [specific] requests known to God. And the peace of God [that peace which reassures the heart, that peace] which transcends all understanding, [that peace which] stands guard over your hearts and your minds in Christ Jesus [is yours].* (Philippians 4:6-7 AMP)

What is peace? Roget's Thesaurus has these words after peace; calm, quiet, stillness, tranquility, silence, harmony and serenity. The word used here in Philippians 4 is defined as one, peace, quietness, rest and set at one again. It is not necessarily the absence of war, but the presence of calmness. Note the Meaning of Peace.

A. The Greek word, "eirene," means "to bind" or "union." The connotation is that where there is a tie that binds, there is peace. The beginning of unity is union. Unity comes when two make peace.

B. The English word, "peace," implies an agreement. Such as a "Peace Treaty." When world leaders want to make peace, they sign a pact, or a treaty. Peace is the result of enemies coming to an agreement.

C. The Hebrew word, "shalom," means may things

be with you the way they ought to be and implies friendship, rest, security. If we have agreement, and we become friends, I am no longer afraid and am now secure. I am now at rest, because he who was my enemy is now my friend, and so we have peace.

Consider these three things that lead to peace in a chaotic world.

1. To experience peace in a chaotic world, you must have a right relationship with God.

Peace with god brings the peace of God. It is a peace that settles our nerves, fills our mind, floods our spirit and, in the midst of the uproar around us, gives us the assurance that everything is all right. *"In everything, by prayer and petition, with thanksgiving, make your requests known to God."*

Our outermost condition may not be changed by this kind of prayer but the love and assurance that such a prayer yields in us opens our hearts to the God of peace. *"Then the peace of God that surpasses all understanding will guard your hearts and minds in Christ Jesus."* This peace must be defended by the thoughts that we let into our minds and hearts.

We must be observant about our thoughts if we are going to preserve that unexplainable peace of God that comes from our relationship with God in Christ Jesus. In the words of Paul, Whatever is true, honorable, just, pure, lovely, gracious, of any excellence, and worthy of praise, think about these things. (Philippians 4:8)

The believer who places his or her full confidence in a loving God and is appreciative in every situation will enjoy a supernatural peace. An inner calm will govern the heart. The faithful believer will know peace—his heart and mind are "protected" by it—despite the tempest raging without.

No one, especially those outside of Christ, will be able to comprehend that peace. To most, it will remain a mystery how someone can be so placid in the midst of turmoil. The peace that comes from being in a right relationship with god is not the peace of this world. The world's peace depends on having favorable circumstances. If things are going well, then we feel peaceful. When things go off-center, the peace quickly dissipates. Jesus made the distinction between His peace and the world's wavering peace. *"Peace I leave with you; my peace I give you. I do not give to you as the world gives."* (John 14:27 NIV)

II. To experience peace in a chaotic world you must learn to remember.

It's easy to assume life would finally be jubilant and a state of satisfaction would be reached if such-and-such happened, or so-and-so came into our lives, or we acquired this or that. The truth is, that isn't the case. But it can be extremely difficult to convince ourselves otherwise.

I want us to remember the peace that God promises us is different than the peace this world has to offer. The peace that appeals to most people hinges on being kind and gentle to them. If they are gentle and smooth, they are at peace. But when difficulties strike, their peace disappears.

The Bible makes it clear that life will be hard. We all will face calamity, conflict, Calvary, and critical times.

But the peace that goes beyond our understanding is based upon remembering that God is present. He doesn't remove the pain and tragedy from our lives, but He does give us peace to live through them. We must remember what Jesus said. *"These thing I have spoken to you, that in Me you may have peace. In the world you will have tribulation; but be of good cheer, I have overcome the world."* (John 16:33, NKJV)

You've got to remember how the story ends. When I buy books, I like to read the last chapter first—because I want to know how the story ends. No matter what I read from the beginning, I read knowing how it's going to end. I sometimes watch Lifetime Movies—and I watch them knowing how it's going to end. The man is going to get knocked out—shot, stabbed or come when everything is over while the woman is going to triumph over the adversity. I like reading the Bible because I know how it's going to end. Remember that the book of Revelation ends with a great Amen, because we win in the end.

III. Finally, to experience peace in a chaotic world, you must learn to rejoice.

"Though the fig tree should not blossom, nor fruit be on the vines, the produce of the olive fail and the fields yield no food, the flock be cut off from the fold and there be no herd in the stalls, yet I will rejoice in the Lord. I will take joy in the God of my salvation. God, the Lord, is my strength..." (Habakkuk 3:17-19, ESV)

We can rejoice indeed because He is the God of our salvation. He has already given Himself over to us. More than the gifts He gives, Jesus, the Giver, is our gift.

Nothing—not sickness, not suffering, not loss—can separate us from this gift.

Paul demonstrates an important lesson. "Our inner attitudes do not have to reflect our outward circumstances." It is easy to be discouraged when we find ourselves in difficult circumstances or to take unimportant events too seriously. As believers we may often find ourselves in circumstances in which we cannot be happy, but we can always rejoice.

Consider the value of rejoicing. On one hand rejoicing eliminates complaining, rejoicing minimizes pouting, rejoicing replaces self-pity and rejoicing diminishes pessimism. On the other hand, rejoicing increases hope, rejoicing refreshes the spirit, and rejoicing validates our testimony. Rejoicing is as much a choice as is griping. Rejoicing is our decision as much as is complaining. Rejoicing is our option as much as moaning. So Paul says choose to rejoice. You can rejoicing when the peace of God is available.

- Rejoice knowing that the God of peace will work in you the Peace of God.
- Rejoice knowing that the God of peace will protect you. (Rom. 16-20)
- Rejoice knowing that the God of peace will be with you. (2 Cor. 13:11)
- Rejoice knowing that the God of peace will sanctify you. (1 Thes. 5;23)
- Rejoice knowing that the God of peace will work in you. (Heb. 13:20-21)

I have been reading up on cruise ships and became aware that modern passenger ships have "stabilizers" that can be run out underwater on each side of the ship to keep the ship from rolling side to side. Let me assure that in rough seas, you will thank God for stabilizers. What stabilizers are to a ship in strong seas, Christ's indwelling Spirit is to the Christian in the storms of life. Imagine, if you will, being stabilized by the gospel. And so to have P-E-A-C-E.

Sometimes you need to grab a P-I-E-C-E of a song, such as the old hymn, "It is Well with My Soul" or "Peace in the Valley" written in 1937.

When you don't feel like singing, grab a P-I-E-C-E of scripture. Cast all your anxiety on Him because He cares for you. 1 Peter 5:7. When the LORD takes pleasure in anyone's way, He causes their enemies to make peace with them. Proverbs 16:7. You will keep in perfect peace those whose minds are steadfast, because they trust in you. Isaiah 26:3. For unto us a child is born, to us a son is given, and the government will be on his shoulders. And he will be called Wonderful, Counselor, Mighty god, Everlasting Father, Prince of Peace. Isaiah 9:6.

Double or Nothing
Rev. Julius L. Jackson,
Macedonia Missionary Baptist Church,
Pastor/Teacher

Text: Matthew 25:19-21

In Max Lucado's book, *Just Like Jesus*, he tells the following story.

"Many years ago a man conned his way into the orchestra of the emperor of China although he could not play a note. Whenever the group practiced or performed, he would hold his flute against his lips, pretending to play but not making a sound. He received a modest salary and enjoyed a comfortable living. Then one day, the emperor requested a solo from each musician. The flutist got nervous. There wasn't enough time to learn the instrument. He pretended to be sick, but the royal physician wasn't fooled. On the day of his solo performance, the impostor took poison and killed himself. The explanation of his suicide led to a phrase that found its way into the English language. *He refused to face the music.*"

You can pretend to be a part of God's orchestra by just blending in and going through the motions. No one notices, because you say the right things, go to the right places, and hang out with the right people. You can enjoy the comfort of being accepted by the crowd of your choice. But there will come a day when you must face the music. One day there is going to be a great separation. On that day you will stand alone before God and give an account for your life, your decisions, and whether or not you were tapped into the living water.

In pursuit of the text, I want to begin with bad news first. Far too many of God's people operate out of fear and are burying their gifts and talents. Consequently, God cannot bless you with increase. Fear is diametric opposite of faith.

- Everything my faith says I can do, fear says I cannot.
- Everything my faith says I can accomplish fear says I will fail.

In fact, fear will apprehend your spirit and traumatize your ability to be creative. It is time to stop the madness and evict fear. Since God has not given us the spirit of fear, why do we continue to rub shoulders with it?

We need to ask ourselves:

- What are you doing with this stress?
- What are you doing with this anxiety?
- What are you doing with these issues?
- What are you doing with these problems?

Listen, you don't have time nor room for fear. God has invested too much in you and expects a return on His investment.

- That Word in you requires a good return.

- That love in you requires a good return.
- That joy in you requires a good return.
- That peace in you requires a good return.
- That inspiration in you requires a good return.

Fear leads to stress. But child of God, remember, you possess too much God in you to be stressed and stretched thin. Fear is a weapon of mass destruction in the devil's arsenal to take you out. But it's time to send that fear back to sender marked addressee unknown.

- Send the devil back his stress!
- Send the devil back his anxiety!
- Send the devil back his issues!
- Send the devil back his problems!
- Send the devil back his confusion!
- Send the devil back his fear!

You ought to establish in your mind: I don't want what the devil sends. What God has for me, is for me and someway, somehow, if I can survive the process, what's coming to me will come. But I'm not going to rush it. I'm not going to get in a hurry. I'm going to do as David suggests in Psalm 40 and *wait patiently on the Lord because after a while he's got to incline His ear unto me and hear my cry.*

The text before us is a lesson in stewardship and accountability. Good stewardship is doing the most with whatever God gives. So as He gives you time, it is your responsibility as a good steward to use it the best you can. Ephesians 5 says *we are to redeem the times.* The New International Version of the same verse says *that we are to make the most of every opportunity,* because the last thing that we want to be is unprofitable. In our text, the benefactor rebuked the man that did not invest. He hid what he had, rather than invest what he had been given.

If you believe God is going to give you an increase, you need to invest in what you believe. You can't expect a harvest where there has been no investment. You've got to put some seed in the ground and know that it is working in your favor. Every farmer knows that a little seed, planted in good soil and well-tended, will produce a harvest exponentially greater than the original seed.

Farmers are meticulous in choosing the right soil. They will till the soil, methodically plant tiny seeds, gently pull away weeds (and let me tell you…the weeds never end!) and anxiously wait for little shoots to come through the dirt. It is rewarding to witness the seedlings emerge and grow into a harvest that we can enjoy.

I believe God has a garden and we are the seeds He chooses to plant. You just have to put something into it. Stop praying

For trees when you're acorns up to ankles. God answered your prayer for the tree when he sent you the acorns. Your thoughts are acorns from which mighty trees emerge. Your talent is given to you to be multiplied.

The truth of the text is based on who knows what and that's what I want to explore.

I. The master knew his people were worthy of his trust.

Her in the parable, I believe the Master and his servants have a common understanding. They both realize that the Master trusted each of them. I don't know about you, but if the Master were to give me a million bucks without so much as a few instructions on what to do with it, I'd seriously consider investing in some crazy stuff.

The question that begs an answer is, of all his servants, why would he choose these three? Because he knows these are all good servants. The Master understands this and gifts each according to his natural ability. Child of god, you have been entrusted with talents because God has deemed you worth of His trust.

II. The Faithful Servants knew their Master trusted them.

Likewise, the faithful servants knew that if the Master saw them as being worthy of stewarding these things, that they ought to live up to that trust.

There's a lot of sermons that boil down to the old cliché, "I wept because I had no shoes, 'til I met the man who had no feet." Well, there's some truth to that, and there's truth to what I've repeated often about how financially blessed we are here in the land of the free and the home of the brave.

But physical things aside, have you ever thought about how blessed we are to be able to read and understand the Bible? Bible Study Worship, and Fellowship—these are all healthy components of a spiritual diet. But what happens if you only feast on the Word and never exercise your faith? Have you ever tried sharing your faith? It's amazing what you'll learn.

III. The lazy servant trusted nothing except himself.

That fatness, that laziness, that inability to use for the Master what is his—that's the real indictment against the last servant. He's not being punished because he somehow lost the things of the Master—but rather because he refused to use them at all. Our God isn't harsh, any more than a doctor is who says, "I prescribed this medicine, why didn't you take it?"

In 2 Peter 1:3, our God has already given us everything we need for life and godliness! By that, we have His Word, a valuable revelation of God Himself. And in that Word, we know that He loves us—so much so that He died for us, taking away our sin and giving us access to God Himself.

So, what is it that makes the faithful servants different from the wicked one? The real difference was this—they knew their Master, and it encouraged them. The lazy servant knew his Master and blamed him. Why? Because ultimately, he refused to see how much his Master truly loved and wanted to invest in him.

The reason we are struggling is because we haven't used resources that God has given. God gives acorns. We invest in that acorn and end up with trees. Despise not the day of small beginnings. You just have to put something into it. Stop praying for trees when you're up in acorns ankles deep. God answered your prayer for the tree when He sent you the acorns. Your thoughts are acorns from which mighty trees emerge. Your talent is given to you to be multiplied. Either you use it, or you lose it.

- How many people have lost their gifts because they have failed to use it?
- How many people have lost their musical ability because they have failed to use it?

- How many people have lost their mathematical genius because they have failed to use it?
- How many people have lost their ability to retain information because they have failed to use it?
- How many people have lost their understanding of the Word because they have failed to use it?

The people that receive the most in life are the people that give the most. As they give, investing in the lives of others they are constantly emptying their hand to be refilled. God gave Adam and Eve specific instructions. He told them to be fruitful, multiply, replenish, subdue, and have dominion. When you bring faith into alignment with God's Word, the message is clear. You become the lender and not the borrower. You become the head and not the tail. You are above and not beneath. You understand Joshua 1:8 (ESV). *"This Book of the Law shall not depart from your mouth, but you shall meditate on it day and night, so that you may be careful to do according to all that is written in it. For then you will make your way prosperous, and then you will have good success."*

- Prosperous is fruitfulness and means to produce an income.
- Prosperous is multiplying and means to make your money grow.
- Prosperous is replenishing and means to restore or reinvest a portion of the profit.
- Prosperous is subduing and means to keep

control of your spending.

The text says that the two that have talents of five and two got more and the one with the one lost it all. I heard Jesus saying "Be faithful over a few things, and I'll make you ruler over many." The race isn't given to the swift nor to the strong, but to the one that holds out and endures to the end. You have got to go through something.

Andre Crouch said it best, through it all, I learned to trust in Jesus and in God.

- I've learned He will provide.
- I've learned He will bring you out.
- I've learned He will bring you through.
- I've learned He will make a way out of no way.
- I've learned how to fast and pray.
- I've learned how to wait on Him.
- I've learned how to depend on Him.
- I've learned how to believe in Him.
- I've learned how to give Him glory.
- I've learned how to wave my hands.
- I've learned how to praise His name.

It's Double or Nothing!
Be not dismayed. Whatever betides,
God will take care of you!

Trapped By Your Own Words
Rev. Leon A. Brumfield
Psalm 34:13-14

Keep thy tongue from evil, and thy lips from speaking guile. Depart from evil, and do good; seek peace, and pursue it.

When someone seeks to capture a lion, that person or persons must use the element of surprise to get his prey. The trap must be positioned at the right location and implemented at the right time. That person must outsmart his prey to be successful. The devil is the master of deception. The devil will set traps so smooth that not only will he capture you, the devil will also capture those persons around you. The devil seeks to steal, kill, and destroy. The devil will steal your joy, kill your spirit, and ultimately seek to destroy you.

How does the devil accomplish such a trap? First the devil will get you following man. The Word says a man must first deny himself, take up his cross and follow after Jesus. Pride is a tool which the devil uses to capture his prey. When a man starts believing that he is all that and a bag of chips, the devil has already won the battle.

Don't you know that Jesus is the Man, we are just

servants? The devil knows that if he can get our attention, he can set up a great fall for us. The devil knows that if he can get our focus away from God, he can damage our spirit.

Take Peter for example. Peter stepped out of that boat and was witnessing a miracle by standing on the water. All was well with Peter until he took his eyes off of Jesus. Then, he began to sink when he notice the boisterous storm. At the end Peter remembered the source of his strength and cried out, "Lord save me."

Jesus picked Peter up and put him back in the boat. Jesus rebuked the wind and the storm ceased. We have some Peters in the house today. You are so quick to step out on faith. Yet, you are so fast to forget the source of your strength.

The devil does not mind the miracles we perform just as long as we forget the miracle-worker. The devil can then set us up for a big fall. When our tongue is in control, the devil already has the victory. James 1:25-26 reads, "But whoso looketh into the perfect law of liberty, and continueth therein, he being not a forgetful hearer, but a doer of the work, this man shall be blessed in his deed. If any man among you seem to be religious, and bridleth not his tongue, but deceiveth his own heart, this man's religion is vain."

You see we deceive ourselves when we don't manage our tongue. The tongue is a little member but so deadly it can kill our spirits and kill spirits around us. Have you ever been around a negative person? If not careful, the negativity will have created a negative outlook with you.

You are what you spiritually eat. When we are always surrounded by negative people, that negative spirit will rub off on us. This constant negative appearance is like feeding our spirits with junk. If all you take in is junk you will soon have a junky spirit. For example, when you are around someone who cusses all the time, you will soon find yourself cussing at times.

In times like these we need a savior. As followers of Christ, it is definitely important that we feed our spirits with the Word. The psalmist said, "Thy word is a lamp unto my feet and a light unto my pathway." The Word will be a solid rock for us to build upon.

There was a parable about two men who built houses. One man built his house on sand and the other man built his house on a solid rock. The man who built his home on sand had the privilege of finishing first and enjoying his home, while it took more time for the man who established his home on a solid rock.

All was well with both men until a storm came. The sand foundation was destroyed by the storm, which uprooted the home. The rock foundation withstood the test of time. Some of us are building our lives on sand. We go by what he says or she says instead of what God has said.

We are trapped by our own words when we feed our spirits with gossip. The theory of the black electrical box is true. Junk in equals junk out. A man is not defiled by what goes into him, but rather what comes out of him. When we allow our lives to be based upon gossip, we are building a bridge on a sand foundation. You wonder why you had that big breakdown. You trusted man instead of God. When we trust in God and never doubt, he will surely bring us out.

Proverbs 3:5-6 says, "Trust in the Lord with all thine heart and lean not to thy own understanding. In all thy ways acknowledge him and He shall direct thy path."

We have too many leaners in our churches today. When the devil brings us a bad report we focus on the negative. As humans we naturally see the hourglass as half empty instead of half full. Why are we that way? We are that way because we are trapped by our own words. We are in bondage to the flesh.

Some of us are serving a life sentence to the flesh. We wonder why we cannot overcome that situation—the reason we are trapped by our own words. Some of us use our minds as garbage collectors. Proverbs 18:21 says, "Death and life are in the power of the tongue: and they that love it shall eat the fruit thereof."

Why are we trapped by our own words? We speak death into our situations instead of life. You care what you eat! We speak death by allowing our minds to feed on the negatives. We kill our spirits by saying words like I cannot do that. We do have a choice, however. Say no to sin and yes to Jesus.

The text says, "Keep thy tongue from evil, and thy lips from speaking guile." This means we must keep our tongues from evil. We have to make an effort to accomplish this feat. In other words, we must manage the mouth. For instance, at work my manager has the responsibility of supervising everyone on my job. The manager knows whether or not I am keeping up with my work based upon my productivity. My manager knows whether I am performing by viewing my work. If the fruit of our labor is in vain, then we will never meet our potential. In our spiritual lives, we have the task of keeping our tongues from evil and that our lips speak no guile. Guile is just the use of tricks to deceive someone.

This task can be measured spiritually by watching our walk. A wolf can disguise himself as a sheep, but his tracks will still be that of a wolf. You can fool your friends some of the time. You can fool your neighbors some of the time. You can fool your spouse some of the time. But, you cannot fool God none of the time. You have to come correct with God. God knows the real deal. God knows when we are going to sin before we even think about it. You have to be careful to not be trapped by your own words.

Being trapped by your own mouth is like walking with shackles on your feet. You will find yourself committing sins over and over again. Say you tried to stop smoking. You might go for a few days, but when the urge to smoke hits you, you give in every time. You may say you said you were going to stop fornicating or having sex outside of marriage, or you are going to stop committing adultery or rather stop being unfaithful to your mate. However, when lust hits, the urge is uncontrollable. You give in every time. You may say you are going to stop being lazy and come to church. Yet, when your head hits the pillow, you oversleep every time. You find yourself being a slave to sin.

Don't worry. You have good company. The Apostle Paul said in Romans 7th chapter beginning with verse 14: "For we know that the law is spiritual: but I am carnal, sold under sin. For that which I do I allow not: for what I would, that do I not; but what I hate, that do I. If then I do that which I would not, I consent unto the law that it is good. Now then it is no more I that do it, but sin that dwelleth in me. For I know that in me (that is, in my flesh,) dwelleth no good thing: for to will is present with me; but how to perform that which is good I find not. For the good that I would I do not: but the evil which I would not, that I do. Now if I do that I would not, it is no more I that do it, but sin that dwelleth in me. I find then a law, that, when I would do good, evil is present with me. For I delight in the law of God after the inward man: But I see another law in my members, warring against the law of my mind, and bringing me into captivity to the law of sin which is in my members." (Romans 7: 14-23)

Paul takes time in Romans to speak about his and our weaknesses. Our flesh is a slave to sin. You wonder why, even though you try with all your might, you are a slave to sin. The reason why is because we are trapped by our own mouths. As long as we are operating in the flesh, we will continue to be trapped and in bondage to sin. However, there is hope nevertheless. We must mortify or die daily to the sin nature. For the spirit wars against the flesh, and the flesh against the spirit. When we abide in the spirit we kill the flesh. When we abide in the flesh we kill the spirit's influence. We are operating any time we are not following God's will. God has a will for each of our lives. We either accept or reject it. As we accept Jesus, we are free from the penalty of sin. As we grown in Christ, we are free from the power of sin. When we go to be with the Lord, we are free from the presence of sin. Whether or not you are dying to the flesh can easily be identified.

Galatians 5:16-24 says, "This I say then, Walk in the Spirit, and ye shall not fulfil the lust of the flesh. For the flesh lusteth against the Spirit, and the Spirit against the flesh: and these are contrary the one to the other: so that ye cannot do the things that ye would. But if ye be led of the Spirit, ye are not under the law. Now the works of the flesh are manifest, which are these; Adultery, fornication, uncleanness, lasciviousness (unwholesome sexual desires), Idolatry, witchcraft, hatred, variance (discord that splits a group), emulations (effort to equal or surpass another), wrath, strife, seditions (dissensions or divisions), heresies (a belief that rejects God), envyings, murders, drunkenness, revellings (rioting), and such like: of the which I tell you before, as I have also told you in time past, that they which do such things shall not inherit the kingdom of God. But the fruit of the Spirit is love, joy, peace, longsuffering, gentleness, goodness, faith, meekness, temperance: against such there is no law. And they that are Christ's have crucified the flesh with the affections and lusts. If we live in the Spirit, let us also walk in the Spirit."

Question: what are you producing, spiritual fruit or works of the flesh?

Here is food for your thoughts. Proverbs 15:2 reads,

"The tongue of the wise uses knowledge aright: but the mouth of fools pours out foolishness."

Psalm 52:2-3 reads, "The tongue devises mischiefs; like a sharp razor, working deceitfully. Thou loves evil more than good; and lying rather than to speak righteousness.

Psalm 59:12 reads, "For the sin of their mouth and the words of their lips let them even be taken in their pride: and for cursing and lying which they speak."

Proverbs 22:12 reads, "The eyes of the Lord preserve knowledge, and he overthroweth the words of the transgressor."

Matthew 12:36-37 reads, "But I say unto you, that every idle word that men shall speak, they shall give account thereof in the Day of Judgment. For by thy words thou shalt be justified, and by thy words thou shalt be condemned."

You don't have to be a slave to sin. You don't have to be trapped by your own mouth. You can be like the Psalmist in Psalms 120:1. "In my distress I cried unto the Lord, and he heard me. Deliver my soul, O Lord, from lying lips, and from a deceitful tongue." Your actions do not want to be at the top of God's hate list. Proverbs 6:16-18 says, "These six things doth the Lord hate: yea, seven are an abomination unto him: A proud look, a lying tongue, and hands that shed innocent blood, a heart that devises wicked imaginations, feet that be swift in running to mischief…"

Are you tired of telling lies to cover lies?

I have good news for you today. There is a God who

sits high and looks low. There is a God who knows what you are going through. This God has been there and experienced all manner of temptations; yet without sin. This God by the name of Jesus Christ thought enough of you and me to leave his heavenly home to suffer so that we do not have to suffer. Christ wrapped himself in human flesh to defeat the devil once for all.

Jesus Christ is the fulfillment of the Old Testament. No longer do you have to be trapped by your own words. No longer do you have to be a slave to sin. You too can have ultimate success through Jesus Christ. Jesus went about doing good. Jesus healed the sick. Jesus gave sight to the blind. Jesus made the lame to walk and the dumb to talk. Jesus offended the Pharisees and Sadducees because their little power was threatened. They beat Him. They spat on him. They called him everything but a child of God. They put a crown of thorns on his head. They pierced Him in his side. Jesus was hung up for our hang ups.

They hung Him high and stretched Him wide. For you and me, for us he died. He died—didn't he die? He stayed dead all night Friday. He stayed dead all night Saturday, but early Sunday morning, He got up with all power in his hands. Black power, economic power, political power, saving power, healing power—all power in his hands.

That's why Jesus is my rock in a weary land. Jesus is my shelter in the time of storm. Jesus—He's joy in the midst of sorrow. Jesus—He's hope for tomorrow. Jesus—He's Ezekiel's wheel in the middle of a wheel. Jesus—

He's my bright and morning star. Jesus—He's the Rose of Sharon. Jesus—He's the lily of the valley. Jesus—He's bread for the hungry. Jesus—He's water for the thirsty. Jesus—He's my breath in the middle of an asthma attack. Jesus—He's peace when I keep tossing and turning at night.

Why don't you free your heart today? Why don't you free your mouth today? Jesus can do it. I know He can. He did it for me.

I was sinking deep in sin, far from the peaceful shore. Very deeply stained within sinking to rise no more. But the master of the sea heard my despairing cry. From the waters lifted me, now safe am I.

What was it? Love lifted me. Love lifted me.

Pure Religion
Bishop Collier Banks

"Pure religion and undefiled before God and the Father is this, to visit the fatherless and widows in their affliction, and to keep himself unspotted from the world." James 1:27

When pure religion is deeply rooted in a heart and life, there will be the upward reach, the inward reach and the outward reach.

I. Pure Religion will reach upward, undefiled before God and the Father.

Christianity is the only pure religion revealed to man by the God of this world. Pure religion must come from above, God is the author of the Christian religion. Those who want to be true Christians must be acquainted with God by the spiritual birth from above by grace through faith in Christ.

The true Christian is a child of God and he will seek earnestly to know the will, the way and the works of God and to please Him in every thought, word and act of life.

Pure religion will react upward by faith and take hold of God and His eternal truth and abide in Him and His truth forever. The true Christian will seek and be able to say, "With Jesus I will always do those things that please Him." Pure religion creates in the heart a passion to be like the Father in love, mercy, holiness, righteousness, grace and goodness.

II. Pure religion will reach inward to keep himself unspotted from the world.

It is the glory of the Christian religion that gives a new heart. It takes away a heart of stone and gives a heart of love. It takes away wickedness and gives righteousness. It gives a new heart with a new conscience to govern it. It gives a new song and a new voice to sing it. It gives new hope and a new faith to reach it. It offers a new home and a new longing to be worthy of it. It gives a new man to walk with a new master.

This is the change Christ makes when he is permitted to enter life. But the better the life the bitter the battle with the sinful world to keep unspotted. Satan seeks to dominate every life, he will try to soil every heart and hand in sin. He would win every way and word for wickedness. He will drag down to ruin every life. Only Christ, who is willing to dwell within, can enable the life to overcome Satan and to keep unspotted from the world.

Do you have Pure Religion?

III. Pure Religion will reach outward.

Visit the fatherless and widows in their affliction. Christianity gives the human heart and life an earnest desire to reach out and help those who are in need. It gives a heart of mercy, tenderness, loving, gracious and helpfulness. The true Christian will desire to give bread to the hungry, water to the thirsty, clothes to the naked, home to the strangers, care to the sick, comfort to the sorrowing, strength to the weak, wisdom to the ignorant, help to the helpless and Christ to the sinner.

In the name of Christ and for the sake of Christ, the Christian will seek to serve for the glory of God.

Seek the Christ of Christianity. Know Him and His way, His will, His Word and His works and love His spirit for His glory.

Bio: Bishop Collier Banks

Bishop Collier Banks is a member of Eleventh Street Baptist Church, Bowling Green, Kentucky, where he serves as Associate Pastor under the leadership of Pastor Carl Whitfield. Bishop Banks is married to Cathey Banks of Shreveport, Louisiana and they are proud parents of five children, one son, four daughters and ten grandchildren.

Bishop Banks was ordained as a minister in 1976 and licensed to preach in 1995. He was consecrated to the office of Bishop by Bishop Paul Morton.

Currently Bishop Banks serves as First Presiding Prelate of the International Bishop Conference and Ministers Fellowship, Inc. (I.B.C.M.F.) under the leadership of Presiding Prelate Bishop Dr. Rickey Moore, Sr. He is a member of the National Assembly of Christian Churches and Ministers Fellowship, Inc. where he serves as Regional Bishop for the states of Tennessee, Kentucky, Ohio, Indiana and Michigan.

Education: *B.A. Degree in Christian Education from Dallas Baptist University, Dallas, TX, graduate of Michigan State University, East Lansing, MI, Master of Divinity from American Baptist College, Nashville, TN and Masters of Theology from Oral Roberts University, Tulsa, OK.*

Professional Experiences: *Bishop Banks has served as Associate Pastor of Sweet Home Baptist Church, Dallas, TX, Associate Pastor Morning Star Baptist Church, Grand Prairie, TX, and served as Pastor of Old Zion Baptist Church, Mt. Clemons, MI and Pastor Substitute at Golden Leaf Baptist Church, Flint, MI.*

His ministerial experience includes pastor/preacher/teacher, Congress of Christian Education Bowling Green, KY, Jail Ministry "Project No Bars," director of Retirement Center Outreach Ministry, Bowling Green, KY and work with the Open Door Drug Ministry-Bowling Green, KY.

He is retired from General Motors Flint, MI and served in the United States Air force.

Bishop Banks declares that he loves the Lord and his main goal is to serve Him and to go where He directs his path.

The Crucifixion of King Self
Bishop Dr. Rickey L. Moore, Sr.

READING: PHILIPPIANS 2:2-5

"Fulfill ye my joy that ye be like minded, having the same love, being of one accord, of one <u>mind</u>. Let nothing be done through strife or vainglory; but in lowliness of <u>mind</u> let each esteem others better than themselves. Look not every man on his own things, but every man also on the things of others. Let this <u>mind</u> be in you, which was also in Christ Jesus."

OVERALL LESSON: PHILIPPIANS 2:1-11

Sometimes your worst enemy is yourself. Many times, you are the person who is blocking your blessings. **King Self** is a descendent from Adam. King Self has a kingdom. His kingdom consists of three: Me, Myself and I. King Self believes he is always right, he likes to have the last word, never wants to be challenged, and is arrogant and self-absorbed.

THE BIBLE TALKS ABOUT THREE ENEMIES
1) The Flesh
2) The World
3) The Devil

"For all that is in the world, the lust of the flesh, and the lust of the eyes, and the pride of life, is not of the

Father, but is of the world." (1 John 2:16)

THE REASON IT IS IMPORTANT TO CRUCIFY KING SELF

When Jesus is on the cross, self is on the throne, but when Self is on the cross, Jesus is on the throne. The throne is your heart and when you accept Jesus as your Savior and King of your place of domicile, He comes in and sets up a kingdom on the front row. He will not force Himself on your throne--you must decrease so that He can increase. In many cases, instead of Jesus being in the center of our hearts, Self is still on the throne.

SELF IN THE FIVE SENSES

1) We hear for *ourselves*
2) See for *ourselves*
3) Taste for *ourselves*
4) Smell for *ourselves*
5) Feel for *ourselves*

We are born into this world selfish. A child has to be taught to share but doesn't have to be taught to be selfish. It is all about I, me and my.

In a marriage, you cannot be selfish. You marry to serve, not to be served. The wife should submit herself to her own husband. Husbands should love their wives as Christ loved the church. As Christ made sacrifices for His church, the husband should make sacrifices for his wife. When you marry you should come off your throne. It is no longer I, me and my. When you put Christ on the throne, the Christ in you will not fight the Christ in each other.

THE EVIDENCE OF KING SELF
- King Self is an individual who is self-centered. It is all about themselves and what they have. *He who puts a fence around himself will always fence out more than he can fence in.*
- Self-seeking
- Self-assertive
- Self-indulgent — full of self-pity
- Self-conscience — always seeking the approval of others
- Self-exalting — wanting to be more than what they really are
- Self-justifying — justifying yourself
- Self-confident — you need to change self-confident to Christ-confident. Luke 22:21, Peter said, "Lord I will never betray you." (He had confidence in himself, but when the pressure was on him, he betrayed Christ.) Unlike Paul who had confidence in Christ. Paul said, "I can do all things through Christ, which strengthens me." (Philippians 4:13)
- Self-willed — I will. In Isaiah 14:13-14 the devil is speaking. He uses the phrase "I WILL" five times.

When Jesus prayed he said, "Father not my will but let thou will be done." When King Self is on the throne your prayer is always *I Will*. When Christ is on the throne of your heart, your conversation is, Father not my Will but your Will be done (Matthew 26:34).

When you are on the throne you see the wrong in everyone but yourself. Many people miss blessings God sends to them because they are caught up in themselves. It is up to us to get "self" off the throne and put Jesus on the throne.

THE BIBLE TALKS ABOUT OTHERS

We should love one another, receive one another, care for one another, (1 Corinthians 12:25) endure one another, have patience with one another, forgive one another (Ephesians 4:32). We find it difficult to forgive, love and have patience with one another when Self is on the throne.

The MIND Concept

In our passage, Philippians 2:2-5, the word mind is used four times. To crucify flesh and put Christ on the throne, we must being with having a **New Mind**. Chapter 2:4-6, a new mind is a selfless mind. Verse 7, a new mind is a serving mind, and in verse 8, a new mind should be a sacrificial mind. We are crucified with Christ but it's Christ that lives in me (Galatians 2:20). Jesus was crucified for us, he expects us to be crucified of ourselves to Him. The first requirement of being a disciple is to deny self (Matthew 16:24).

Sunday, February 8, 2015
Bishop Dr. Rickey Moore, Sr.

"Lift Every Voice and Sing"

Psalm 137, Verses 1-4 Foundation

Connecting to the love Poem, titled, "Lift Every Voice and

Sing"

When Asaph wrote this song, he put the spotlight on the dark period of Israel when they were slaves, captives of the Babylonians.

"By the rivers of Babylon, there we sat down, yea, we wept, when we remembered Zion. We hanged our harps upon the willows in the midst thereof. For there they that carried us away captive required of us a song; and they that wasted us required of us mirth, saying, sing us one of the songs of Zion. And they responded, how shall we sing the Lord's song in a strange land?" Psalms 137:1-4

THE HISTORY

The song: "Lift Every Voice and Sing, was chosen to be the National Negro Anthem. James Weldon Johnson and his brother John wrote the song.

James and his brother worked in New York, writing and producing plays on Broadway. When James returned to his home in Jacksonville, Florida, he became principal of his hometown school. Some of his students wanted to honor President Abraham Lincoln on his birthday because he was instrumental in freeing the slaves. James Weldon Johnson wrote a poem to be recited on that day that talked about the painful past of the American people. His brother John, who was a musician added music to the song, and they decided that it would be more effective to pass the poem on to the young people and have them sing it rather than for it to be read by James Weldon Johnson as a poem. According to history, it was song by a 500-voice choir.

This song had a unique journey of many transitions.

It began as a poem and later became a song. The third stanza of this song is a prayer. Today it is an anthem.

THERE ARE FIVE THINGS THE AUTHOR GAVE TO THE PEOPLE OF COLOR THROUGH THIS SONG:

1) **Challenges to sing in spite of suffering.** Trouble, pain, heartbreak, and heartache will give you a song. "Lift Every Voice and Sing" reminds us we can sing in spite of. Do not sing low but sing loud, "Ring with the harmonies of liberty, Let our rejoicing rise, high as the listing skies. Let it resound loud as the rolling sea." In the Bible each time someone went through a tragedy, they had a song. When they went through the Red Sea and Pharaoh's army came after them, Miriam started to sing, "Guide me thy great Jehovah pilgrim through this barren land." While Israel was held captive, they thought about how good God had been to them and they sang. When Paul and Silas were in jail, they sang. In the upper room after the Lord's Supper, they, including Jesus, sang a song, and they went out.

2) **There is expectation in spite of the experience.** We are "facing the rising sun of a new day begun." Thank God, for faith, hope and love. Faith aspires me, hope assures me and love is me.

3) **Reminds us that we as a people have a painful past.** Young people should talk to their parents and grandparents about the painful past of our people. About the times when there were white and colored water fountains and restrooms. Having to sit at the back of the bus, our people attacked by dogs at the command of police officers. During the time, Johnson wrote the words

to the song, there was a painful past: One hundred and five people had been lynched. He wrote the song 35 years after the enslaved people gained their freedom in 1865, and 43 years after the Dred Scott Decision (a case in which the U.S. Supreme Court ruled that a slave (**Dred Scott**) who had resided in a Free State and territory (where slavery was prohibited) was not entitled to his freedom. "God of our weary years, God of our silent tears, Thou who has brought us thus far on the way."

4) Not only do we have a painful past but also, we have a fruitful future. When you go through something, if it was not fatal, that means it was not final, and you can be forgiven, and you can still have a future because of the forgiveness and the faithfulness of your heavenly father. There is a fruitful future.

5) There is praise for his divine presence. No matter what we go through, the God we serve is always there.

Bio: Bishop Dr. Ricky L. Moore, Sr.

A native of Shreveport, Dr. Moore is a third-generation pastor, the grandson of the Rev. J. J. Jones and the great-grandson of the late Rev. John Jefferson Jones (the Black Billy Sunday). Dr. Moore resides in Shreveport, Louisiana with his wife Sharon and their son Rickey Moore, Jr. He has been providing dedicated service, commitment and labors of love to the Sunrise Baptist Church Family since 1998.

He began his studies in Theology at Wiley College in Marshall, Texas and earned his undergraduate degree from Bishop College in Dallas, Texas. He holds an Honorary PhD from Stetson Christian College, Akin, SC. He has earned six doctorate degrees: Doctor of Divinity, Doctor of Ministry, Doctor of Humanities, Doctor of

Theology, Doctor of Law of the Old Testament and Doctor of Distinguished Service Award, from Baptist Theological Seminary.

Bishop Dr. Ricky L. Moore, Sr. is a compassionate pastor who is a devoted, humble servant of God, a dynamic preacher and a prolific teacher. The church is blessed to be benefactors of his Christ-centered leadership.

Dr. Moore epitomizes the true meaning of the scripture, "Preach the Word; be instant in season, out of season; reprove, rebuke, exhort with all longsuffering and doctrine." II Timothy 4:2

His greatest joy is "Sharing his passion for preaching."

Sermon Notes: Bishop Dr. Rickey L. Moore, Sr.

Jesus' Last Teachings
St John 13:34-35
The New Commandment

A.   *The new commandment specified in this chapter is one of the greatest attractions of Christianity.*

B.   *To make sure that the Disciples understood what He was telling them, Jesus demonstrated the attitude that they were to have with each other. He realizes that unless His followers love each other and demonstrated it, the Church would not survive.*

In St. Luke 22:24, the disciples argued over who was the greatest. Love does not care who is the greatest, so Jesus focuses on that. It has been said that Love is the essence of the divine nature and since God is love and to have His nature, love should be our nature as well.

I. The New Commandment Jesus gives is found in John 13:34.
   A. The Ten Commandments are 80% negative.
      1. This commandment is totally positive and enables one to keep all of the laws of Moses.
      2. This commandment makes it simple to please God as well as to live the Christian life.

B. No one can rightfully claim to be God's child who does not keep all of the commandments, including this one.
  1. The very nature of Christianity is that we are imitators of Christ.
  2. If we do not keep His commandments, we do not love Him and are not His followers. John 14:15 says, "If you love me, keep my commandments".
C. Love is the genuine stamp of purity in Christianity.
  1. Some people are kind, good neighbors and love others—the problem is they don't love God. So, they are not keeping all of the commandments.
  2. Some people profess to be Christians but do not live warm, loving lives. Since God's nature is not theirs, they are not His.
  3. Love for God and for others is the distinguishing mark of discipleship.
  4. A person can be religious without love but cannot be a Christian without love. It's like the difference between gold-plated jewelry and pure, gold jewelry.
D. Love enables us to fulfill all the other commandments. It deliberately practices that which pleases the one love.

II. John 13:1-5, Jesus demonstrates how to show love
  A. Service is the language of love. In this passage, Jesus took the role of a servant and washed his

disciples' feet. Jesus shielded Judas from exposure because He loved him. He demonstrated His love for you and me by going to the cross.

B. Love is something that you do. Ruth expressed her love for Naomi by staying with her. Jacob proved his love for Rachel by working for 14 years. In Jesus' conversation with Peter in John 21, He told Peter to show Him that he loved Him. Love is still evidenced by actions, rather than by words.

Conclusion

I Corinthians 13, emphasizes the characteristics of love, by living this way, we can be sure we are keeping the commandments. If we love God, or lives will show that love. It is easy to be a Christian. We must love God and do what comes naturally.

PASTOR DAVID T. FERRELL, D.TH.
BIOGRAPHY

David T. Ferrell is a native of Marshall, Texas. David was raised by his father and mother. His father was a preacher and his mother a homemaker. They helped their children develop a reverence and love for God at an early age.

As a teenager, David united with the Macedonia Baptist Church under the leadership of the late Reverend Ray Horton. It was through Pastor Horton's leadership, teaching and preaching the Holy Spirit began to operate in David's life.

David eventually moved to Fort Worth, TX. This move would lead David to make some major decisions concerning the direction of his life. David entered into matrimony and also united with

Paradise Missionary Baptist Church, pastored by the late J.L. Singleton. It was at Paradise, God would begin calling David.

As with Jonah, Jeremiah and some other Prophets, David was hesitant about yielding to the call. However, after an accident where David broke his leg and nearly had it amputated, David would say, "Speak Lord, your servant is listening." The Lord had an opportunity to minister to David – it was at this time he heeded the Master's call.

David finally began his vocation by serving as an usher, singing in the choir, and performing other duties to support the work of the Kingdom. God saw David's sincerity and faithfulness to the kingdom, and decided to call David to a greater position in the Kingdom – to preach His uncompromising Gospel. God confirmed David's call by giving him the gift of oration. David would stand boldly and proclaim God's Word with conviction and confidence.

To enhance his call to preach the Gospel, David enrolled in classes at Southwestern Theological Seminary where he earned a certificate in biblical studies. He continued his studies and enrolled in New World Bible Institute, where he earned a Bachelor of Theology Degree. After graduating from New World Bible Institute, David enrolled at Trinity Baptist Bible College where he earned a Master of Divinity and Doctor of Divinity Degrees.

David T. Ferrell is a life-long learner, who continues to dive into the treasures of God's Word. He currently serves as Pastor of Galilee Missionary Baptist Church, Venus, TX, where he has served for 45 years. David serves as an instructor and preacher at various associations and congresses on the local, state, and national level. He serves with the Ministers Against Crime, and formerly, with the Coalition for Justice Organization. David continues to be a positive influence to many. He mentors young ministers and is skilled at providing wise counsel. David is a great gift to the Body of Christ.

Resolutions & Hints for the Church

Baptist Church Officers and Staff Duties and Responsibilities

CHAIRMAN OF DEACONS:

The Chairman of the Deacons above all the Church officers, should have the program of the Church at heart. He should be sincere in his dealings in the affairs of the Church and not be swayed by every wind and doctrine and everyone who comes along.

The Chairman should also be a LEADER in the stewardship program in the Church, giving of his time, his talent, service and tithes in support of the Church.

The Chairman likewise should be FILLED WITH THE HOLY SPIRIT, FAITHFUL, EXPERIENCED IN THE WORK OF THE CHURCH AND A DEVOUT CHRISTIAN!

His Duties and Responsibilities Are:

1. Be able to work with the Pastor in the responsibility of deaconship.
2. Be able to organize the deacons to get the jobs of the deacons done.
3. Serve as moderator for deacon meetings.
4. Build agendas for Deacons' meetings with the

approval of the Pastor.
5. Coordinate all organized deacon activity primarily centered on the family care ministries.

DEACONS:

The first Deacons were chosen to look after the daily ministration of common funds in order that the Apostles might have more time for prayer and the ministry of the Word. But they were also to be SPIRITUAL LEADERS in the church.

The Deacons are to be the Pastor's helpers in all the activities of the Church—his assistants in carrying on the great work of the Master.

Deacons are ordained and should always be men of HONESTY, SPIRITUALITY AND WISDOM. Men are only recommended for this office whose lives and examples as Christians are considered satisfactory by the Church. (Acts 6:1-7, 1 Timothy 3:8-13)

The principal duties of the Deacons consist of administering the temporal affairs of the Church. These include the relief of the poor, the support of public worship, the care of the Church property and the proper provision for the due administration of the ordinances. *To serve the "TABLES":*
1. The Table of the Poor
2. The Table of the Church
3. The Table of the Pastor

The Pastor, however, is the shepherd, the guide, the overseer of the entire Church, and he should always be recognized as such by the Deacons, who are only his assistants, as well as by the rest of the Church.

CHAIRPERSON OF THE DEACONESS:

This person is a woman of strong Christian integrity and firm in the belief and doctrine of the Church. She is also one who supports her Church with much prayer and sincerity.

Her Duties and Responsibilities Are:
1. Organize Deaconess Committee to do the work of the Deaconess.
2. Cooperate with Pastor and Deacons in all work of the Church.

TRUSTEES:

Trustees should be individuals who are concerned about the welfare and progress of the Church—both as a religious and spiritual organism and also as a physical plant.

The Responsibilities of This Office Are:
1. Being a good steward in the support of the Church in every way.
2. Representing the Church in legal matters according to the law.
3. Taking constant checks of the Church building to sense the needs.
4. Knowing business transactions and procedures.

CHURCH CLERK:

The office of the Church Clerk is one of the most important offices of the Church. The person selected for

this office should:
1. Know how to keep accurate records and how to present these records economically and attractively.
2. Be regular in attendance, interested in every phase of the Church's life, quick to perceive the difference between essentials and non-essentials, reliable and trustworthy.
3. The Church Clerk is more than a recorder of minutes of business meetings. The Church Clerk is the Church's HISTORIAN.
4. Keep membership roll in good order.
5. Keep records of letter of dismissals.
6. Keep records of baptismals, Christian experience, etc.
7. Work with Pastor in development of other materials and correspondence when needed.

ASSISTANT CHURCH CLERK:

The same duties apply in the absence of the Church Clerk.

FINANCIAL SECRETARY:

The office of Financial Secretary is a very important office. One who serves in this important position should be trustworthy, character and integrity unquestionable, and a good steward in the tithing program of the Church.

The Person in This Position Will be Responsible For:
1. Knowing business and bookkeeping and be very accurate in keeping records.
2. Sharing in counting the money and recording each

individual gift.
3. Keeping detailed accounts of all receipts and expenditures.
4. Prepare Financial Bulletin each month for the members of the Church.

TREASURER:

The office of Treasurer is an important position in the Lord's Church.

One who serves in this position should be honest, character and integrity unquestionable, and devoted to the cause of Christ.

This Person Will be Responsible For:
1. Helping to count the Lord's money.
2. Making deposits of the Lord's money into the bank in appropriate checking accounts.
3. Receiving the Monthly Financial Report from each auxiliary.

BUILDING FUND SECRETARY:

The Building Fund Secretary is responsible for preparation and maintenance of all Church Building Fund Records and Reports.

Specifically, the Job May Include:
1. Maintain record of all receipts and disbursements of Building Fund.
2. Post individual offering records for Building Fund efforts.
3. Reconcile monthly bank statements.

4. Prepare Monthly Building Fund Reports
5. Maintain records of purchase orders, invoices, etc.
6. Prepare checks for approved expenditures.
7. Perform other responsibilities as assigned for the Building Fund.

ASSISTANT BUILDING FUND SECRETARY:

The Assistant Building Fund Secretary will be in charge of Special Building Fund efforts. The same duties will apply in the absence of the Building Fund Secretary.

MUSICIAN:

A Church Musician should be a person of true Christian character and firm conviction, having a working knowledge of church music, a playing knowledge of instruments used in church worship services, and have a general oversight and direction of the music.

The Responsibilities of This Office Are:
1. Providing worshipful music for all Services and Departments of the Church.
2. Lead all choirs in practices and rehearsals at their scheduled times.
3. Cooperate with the Pastor in the selection of new music and arrangements to be used in the worship service.
4. Attend District, State or National Meetings to receive information that will upgrade the overall Music Department.

ASSOCIATE MUSICIANS:

The Associate Musicians shall help in the total up-building of the Music Department, to assist during and in the absence of the Musician.

WOMEN MISSIONARY UNION PRESIDENT(S):

The President of the Mission should be a woman with definite spiritual convictions and interested in mission work. One who loves her Church and cooperates fully with its program. One who is able to work with the Pastor in the progressive program of the church. She should be friendly, tactful, thoughtful and have leadership ability.

Her Responsibilities Are:
1. Preside at meetings of the WMU.
2. Prepare agenda for each meeting to avoid loss of time.
3. Work with the Circle Leaders and Youth Leaders in the work of the WMU.
4. Keep the program of the church before all mission sisters at all times.
5. Cooperate with the Pastor in promoting the total program of the church.
6. Lead out in the stewardship program of the Mission Society.
7. Attend District, State and National Meetings, if possible, in order to be informed on Mission work which will benefit our own WMU Program.

YOUTH DIRECTRESS:

The Youth Directress should be a person with definite spiritual convictions and interested in children of all ages. One who loves her church and the growth of her church. She should be a person who knows how to organize programs for young people.

Responsibilities Are:
1. Preside at all meetings.
2. Cooperate with Pastor and church programs.
3. Attend District, State and National Meetings, if possible, to be informed on the advancement of Youth Work.

SUPERINTENDENT OF CHURCH SCHOOL:

This individual is the chief administrative officer of the Teaching Department who has definite spiritual convictions, sincere concern for the progress of the church and have a fair knowledge of scriptures and their application.

The Responsibilities of This Office Are:
1. Organize staff sufficient to meet the needs of the Church School.
2. Enlist and train teachers as needed.
3. Work cooperatively with the Pastor on the overall Church School Program.
4. Lead every Department of the Church school in sincere worship and stewardship.
5. Attend meetings, if possible, District, State and National to gain information that can help to

promote our Church School Program.

BAPTIST TRAINING UNION DIRECTRESS:

This person is an individual with vision and must have objectives and leadership ability, unquestioned loyalty to her Church and Pastor.

The Responsibilities of This Position Are:
1. Work cooperatively with Pastor in keeping the program of the Church before the people.
2. Lead the Training Union in a sincere stewardship program.
3. Attend District, State or National Meetings, if possible, to help promote our Training Union Program.

CHAIRMAN OF USHERS:

The President of the Ushers should be a person of true Christian character and conviction, have leadership ability and be a good organizer, have a sincere, pleasant personality, show a concern for Christ and His work, concern for worship services, people and orderliness.

The Responsibilities of This Office Are:
1. Be able to organize the Ushers and hold regular meetings for business and drills in the name of the Lord.
2. Lead the Ushers in a stewardship program in Church work.
3. Work cooperatively with the Pastor in keeping the program of the Church before the Members and

Ushers.
4. Be a good public relations person.
5. Attend District, State and National Meetings, if possible, to get information that will be useful and help promote the program of the Ushers.

BROTHERHOOD PRESIDENT:

This person is a leader and organizer of men and boys in the Church. He should have strong convictions about the Church and the doctrines of the Church. He should also be sincere in his Christian duties and above all, possess leadership ability and have a fair understanding and knowledge of brotherhood organization.

This Person Has the Responsibility Of:
1. Organizing the men and boys to do the work of their organization.
2. Keeping the program of the Church before the men at all times.
3. Cooperating with the Pastor in promoting the program of the Church.
4. Leading the men in a sincere stewardship program in the Church.
5. Attending District, State or National Meetings, if possible, to promote the Layman Program in our Church.

CHOIR PRESIDENT(S):

The President of the Choir should have a fair knowledge of people and all groups in the Music Department. The Music Department as an organization should have business meetings apart from rehearsals, once a month or special call meetings when necessary.

The Responsibilities of This Office Are:
1. Prepare an agenda for all business meetings of the Choir and preside at all meetings.
2. Organize Choir to carry out their work in the Church and attend rehearsals "ON TIME."
3. Have regular attendance at both services (Morning and Evening Worship).
4. Keep the program of the Church before the Choir at all times.
5. Lead the Music Department in a sincere stewardship program.

CHURCH HOSTESS:

A Church Hostess is Chairperson of the Kitchen committee.

The Responsibilities of This Office Are:
1. Have a great concern and love for the Church.
2. Formulate policies of the kitchen and for communicating those policies to Church members.
3. Formulate policies for the use of the kitchen by all auxiliaries of the Church.
4. Have a fair knowledge of food services, cost and preparations.

5. Keep supplies in kitchen with the help of the Kitchen Committee, along with sanitation of the kitchen.
6. Cooperate with the Pastor in the work of the Church.

DECORATION COMMITTEE:

The Chairperson of the Decoration Committee should be a person who is able to work with all organizations of the Church in a Christian spirit.

The Responsibilities of This Office Are:
1. To work with the Pastor upon special request for any decoration of other areas of the Church.
2. Will decorate for the following special occasions: Church Anniversary, Pastor's Anniversary, Christmas and changing of seasonal arrangements.
3. Willing to help other Departments upon request for decorations.
4. Will be responsible for decoration supplies and turning in all charges upon receipt.

Helpful Tools for the Church

Litany of Dedication

Minister: In recognition of the Great commission which bids us. "Go-make-disciples-baptize-teach" and in harmony with the message, which reads that "Jesus advanced in wisdom in stature and in favor with God and man." We come to this moment of dedication praying that blessings in everlasting abundance may prevail in the hearts of all who have made this happy moment possible. To the sowing of the good seed of the kingdom in the hearts of all of our people, young and old.

Officers: We dedicate ourselves to the service of God Almighty.

Minister: In the train of the man of Galilee who was God's example of the mastery of life, and who calls us to come up ever higher in personal purity and strive toward perfection, as our Father in Heaven is perfect.

Officers: We yield our will to His will and pray for power to follow in His footsteps.

Minister: In the spirit of the Carpenter of Nazareth who was of good report in every affair of business and who brought dignity to honest toil by devoting its rewards to good and a nobler life.

Officers: We take as ours His dream of the Kingdom of God on Earth in our work and in our worship.

Minister: In the faith of Him who drew a circle embracing all men and nations as the children of God and who prayed that all might be one, to the end that the world may believe.

Minister: To the officers and members of *New Hope Baptist Church (insert your church name)*, what do you pledge in the year of our Lord *(current year)*?

Officers and Members:
I covenant with God:
1. To be present at the communion table and regular church services and to endeavor to induce other members to do likewise.
2. To recruit men, women, boys and girls for Christ by winning them through personal contact and invitation to attend church.
3. To support the work of the church at home and to the uttermost parts of the world.

Prayer: Pastor

Hymn: "Have Thine Own Way"

Jesus Christ Is...

Jesus Christ is...
Abel's Sacrifice, Noah's Rainbow, Abraham's Lamb, Isaac's Well, Jacob's ladder, Ezekiel's Burden, Judah's Scepter, Moses' Rod. David's Slingshot, Hezekiah's Sundial.

Jesus Christ is...
A Husband to the Widow.
A Father to the Orphan.
To those traveling in the dark night, He is the Bright and Morning Star.
To those in the lonesome valley, He is the Lily of the Valley, the Rose of Sharon, Honey in the Rock and the Staff of Life.
He is the Pearl of Great Price
He is the Rock in a Weary Land
He is the Counselor
He is the Everlasting Father, and the government of our lives is on his shoulder.
He is Peter's Shadow and John's Pearly White City.
He is Jesus...Jesus of Nazareth. Son of the Living God!

Jelly Bean Prayer
Contributed by Angela Techecko

Have you heard the story of the jelly beans?
The black ones are a symbol of our sinful heart,
cold and hard not a good start. The red ones would
be the blood shed for you and me. The white ones
would mean washed white as snow, by the blood
of Jesus do you know?
The green ones mean
growth for our clean heart, so we can tell others of
Jesus, now that's a good start.
The yellow ones would mean streets of gold,
like the ones in Heaven, as in the book of
Revelation is told. The purple ones are to mean like
the robe He wore,
when our sins on the cross He bore.
So the next time you see a bag of jelly beans,
you will know what the colors mean.

RED is for the blood He gave.
GREEN is for the grass He made.
YELLOW is for the sun so bright.
ORANGE is for the edge of night.
BLACK is for the sins we made.
WHITE is for the grace He gave.
PURPLE is for His hour of sorrow.
PINK is for our new tomorrow.

You Blessed Me!
By: Rev. Leon A. Brumfield
Asst. Editor for ERRP

Lord, you blessed me (blessed me)
Brought me through dangers seen and unseen
You blessed me with the victory.
My concerns are now history.

You picked me up with Your Almighty hands.
When I was sinking in the sands
Lord, You are my everything
You blessed me with visions and dreams
You are the source of all my needs
In my heart, You planted this seed
All praises to Your holy name
My life will never be the same.

I was sinking deep in my sins.
Father, You told me I could win.
You cleansed this old sinner
And made me a winner
Now, I'm blessed by Your grace.
I told the devil - get out of my face
I rebuked him that very hour
By Your Almighty power

I realize You are my all in all
You caught me before a fall
My name is in the Lamb's Book of Life
You traded all of my strife
Gave me love, joy and peace

Albert Van Fisher

These gifts I cannot receive from a priest
Now, my entire life has changed.
You took my heart and rearranged.

"What Kind of Man Am I?"
Written by Delonzo Starks

I try my best to do what's right, but sometimes I slip, like a thief, in the night.
(What kind of man am I?)
I know the feeling, when I do wrong, I ask the Lord for forgiveness, to help me carry on.
(What kind of man am I?)
The love in my heart, that is here to stay, but curiosity, sometimes gets in the way.
(What kind of man am I?)
Am I the kind of man, that will make people believe or am I the kind of man that will try to deceive. I pray every night on my hands and knees, I ask the Lord for strength to help comfort me. The first person in life, you hurt is yourself, then confusion sets in, and makes you think of everyone else.
(What kind of man am I?)
The longer I live the more I try to understand, is this the best that I can do, to call myself a man? Most of the time, I can say, I feel glad, but some of the things that I do, it just makes me mad.
(What kind of man am I?)
When my time has passed and comes judgment day, I pray that the Lord will see, that I come his way.
I pray.

Let Freedom Ring

From every mountainside, *let freedom ring*. When we *let freedom ring*, when we *let freedom ring* from every village and every hamlet, from every state and every city, we will be able to speed up that day.

I have a *dream*...Let *freedom* ring!

Excerpt from "I Have a Dream Speech"

This will be the day when all of God's children will be able to sing with a new meaning, "My country, 'tis of thee, sweet land of liberty, of thee I sing. Land where my fathers died, land of the pilgrim's pride, from every mountainside, let freedom ring." And if American is to be a great nation this must become true.

***Excerpts from Dr. Martin Luther King Jr. used under Fair Use Laws. The entire speech is protected by US Copyright, but can be found online at www.archives.gov/files/press/exhibits/dream-speech.pdf

As authors and Christians, we must always uphold governing laws and respect the copyright of others. Please feel free to look up the full content of this wonderful speech, but do not infringe on copyright when publishing any part of it whether for general publication or in church bulletins, newsletters or other printed materials.

Strategies for Improving Memory

1. **PAYING ATTENTION:** Concentrating and focusing in on information is always the first step towards remembering it. Make an effort to listen and process the information. Do not "half listen."
2. **ENVIRONMENT CONTROL:** As much as possible, eliminate distractions when listening or trying to remember. (Turn off the TV, close your eyes, clear your mind, etc.)
3. **VERIFICATION:** Verify the information with the person giving it to you. Ask for repeats if you didn't hear it. Repeat the information back to them.
4. **REHEARSAL:** Repeat the information over and over to yourself.
5. **VISUALIZATION:** Close your eyes and picture the information in your head (See yourself doing it, make a mental map, picture the object, etc.)
6. **ORGANIZATION:** Organize the information into smaller units. For example, instead of trying to remember seven (7) numbers for a phone number, remember it as three (3) numbers followed by four (4) numbers. Another example: instead of remembering a random list for the store, remember it in categories (by the aisle #, by the type of product, etc.).
7. **ASSOCIATION:** Remember something by associating it with something else that is more meaningful to you or easier to remember. For

example, you can remember someone's name by associating their name with someone else you know, a rhyming word, or a physical word, or a physical feature of that person.
8. **WRITE IT DOWN:** Leave notepads and pencils by the phone, keep an appointment book with you, make to do lists, etc.

Are you Stepping Out for Christ Jesus?

WHAT WILL YOUR ANSWER BE?

I hope your answers to those two questions were, "Yes!"

However, if you were undecided there is no pressure, because Jesus Christ is a gentleman, and it's your choice.

The Lord Jesus is knocking at your heart's door right now, but He will not come in until you invite Him in. Caution: I must warn you, just don't wait too long.

In Saint John chapter 9 verse 4, it reads, "I must work the works of him that sent me, while it is day: the night cometh, when no man can work."

There are many things that might occur in your life that could hinder you from making the right choice, or death comes.

Matthew chapter 12, verse 30 reads, "He that is not with me is against me."

Now for those of you whose answers were yes, you have taken the STEP OF FAITH to receive Jesus Christ personally as Your Savior. Because of this choice, you have the opportunity to gain eternal life, the gift of God through Jesus Christ His Son.

Saint John chapter 3, verse 36 reads, "He that believeth on the Son hath everlasting life: and He that believeth not the Son shall not see life; but the wrath of God abideth on him." Once again I remind you that Jesus said, "behold, I stand at the door, and knock: if any Man hear my voice, and open the door, I will come in to him, and will sup with him, and he with me." (Revelation

3:20) When Jesus says, "behold, I stand at the door," He is speaking about the very door of your heart.

Prayer

Lord Jesus, believing I am lost and separated from you by my sins, I am willing to turn from my sins. I receive you as the Savior and Lord of my life. I thank you, Lord Jesus for coming into my life as you.

STEPS to a life of blessings:
 Belong to God's family (John 3:1-3)
 Keep His commandments (Titus 2:11-12)
 Humble yourself (James 4:6)
 Give generously (2 Corinthians 9:6-9)
 Love one another (John 13:34-45)
 Strive for unity (Psalm 133)
 Forgive others (Mark 11:25-26)

Lose everything but your faith in God and you'll lose nothing—lose your faith in God and you'll lose everything!

My Prayer to the Lord

I pray that the Almighty Lord Jesus pour out the choicest blessings into your life. I pray that the Lord would heal all of your loved ones who are suffering from sicknesses and diseases. I pray that the Lord would illuminate your understanding, so that you can unlock the hidden treasures the Lord has for you this year.

It is my prayer that you receive knowledge from the Word of God that will open new doors of opportunity. I pray that your family members who do not know God would come to know God in a special way.

Lord, I am reminded like Jeremiah that nothing is too hard for You! Lord, I thank You for who You are and whose we belong to. Lord, I pray that the indwelling Spirit would abide in us daily. I pray for strength for people to resist the temptations of the devil. Lord, I pray that as we rise to new levels this year that we always put You first.

I know that apart from You we can do nothing. I pray that You walk with us so closely that we feel Your divine presence. Lord, I pray for our leaders in the community, city, state, nation, and world that You would guide them to make godly decisions. Lord, I pray for us to have holy boldness to be a witness of You on our jobs, social activities, and neighborhoods.

I pray that as we close chapter 2015 that we do not carry over the baggage that weighs us down in 2016. I pray that You would forgive us for all our sins, and separate them as far as the east is from the west.

May You Be Blessed By the Lord Jesus Christ Till We Meet Again!

In the name of our Lord and Savior I pray — Amen.

Editor's Note: Although this prayer was written in 2015, it is a timeless prayer, applicable for the ending of any year. The truths penned in Dr. Fisher's prayer remain as relevant in current days as they did when he wrote them and dating back in time to the prophet he mentions. May this prayer remind each person reading this book of the blessings God offers to all who follow Him with all of their hearts, souls and minds.

The Holy Alphabet

Although things are not perfect
Because of trial or pain
Continue in thanksgiving
Do not begin to blame
Even when times are hard
Fierce winds are bound to blow
God is forever able
Hold on to what you know
Imagine life without His love
Joy would cease to be
Keep thanking Him for all the things
Love imparts to thee
Move out of "Camp Complaining"
No weapon that is known
On earth can yield the power
Praise can do alone
Quit looking at the future
Redeem the time at hand
Start every day with worship
To "thank" is a command
Until we see him coming
Victorious in the sky
We'll run the race with gratitude
Xalting God most high
Yes, there'll be good times and yes some will be bad, but...
Zion waits in glory...where none are ever sad

Talk with God
Zora Guntharp

There are times when I get blue
And hardly know just what to do,
Then God takes me by the hand
And says, "My child, I understand.

When you have a troubled mind,
Just talk to me and you will find
I will be with you all the day
Leading and guiding in every way.

When troubles run so very high
Always know that I am nigh
Just call on me and you will see
A happier person you will be.

Be patient, my child, do not despair
Remember I am always there
Loving and caring every day
As you trod along life's way.

When nights are long and pleasures are few
Stop and listen, I'll tell you what to do
Trust in me for all things too
And I will always see you through."

Note from author: I was inspired to write this poem when I first got sick in 1982. Now it's 1995, and I will be 80 this year. I pray this poem will be a blessing to all who read it. May it encourage you to keep trusting in the Lord.

The Church Must Believe These Things
The Church Must Believe THE BIBLE
Reverend Charlie H. Foy

WHAT IS THE BIBLE?
1. The Bible is the book of books.
2. The Bible is the only authentic source from which instructions can be derived in relationship to the knowledge of God.
3. The Church must believe that Jehovah God is the maker and supreme ruler of Heaven and Earth. (Genesis 1:1)
4. The Church must believe that God is worthy of all possible honor, confidence and love.
5. The Bible was written by men who were divinely inspired by the Holy Spirit. (II Samuel 23:1-4 and
6. I Peter 1:19-21)
7. The Bible is a perfect treasure of Heavenly Instructions, with God as its author, salvation for its end, and the truth without any mixture of error. (II Timothy 3:16-17)
8. The Church must believe that the Godhead consists of three personalities, God the Father, God the Son and God the Holy Spirit, equal in every divine perfection and executing distinct, but harmonious offices in the great work of redemption. (Romans 1:19-20)
9. The Church must believe that there is only one true and living God, who is an infinite and intelligent Spirit. (Ps 147:5) (St John 4:23-24)

10. The Bible was written for man's benefit. (Romans 15:4-6)

CHURCH, YOU MUST BELIEVE IN GOD.
IF YOU BELIEVE...SAY AMEN!

Family Rules

Keep your promises.
Share
Think of others before yourself.
Say I Love You.
Listen to your parents.
Do your best.
Say Please And Thank You.
Always Tell The Truth.
Hug Often
Laugh at yourself.
Use Kind Words
Love Each Other.

Tributes to Pastor Fisher

Blessed of the dead, which die in the Lord from here forth: yeah saith the Spirit — that they may rest from their labors; and their works do follow them.

It Was Not Just About

Because you cared for me, I have been blessed to care for you. Hoping that I have done you proud in all I've tried to do. I have been blessed to be on this journey with you called the cycle of life when the caregiver becomes the cared for.

Daddy, even though we have not always seen eye to eye, I wouldn't give anything for the trials we have been through.

It was Not just about the trip, but it was the journey.

It was Not just about what I took, it was about what you gave.

It was Not just about the disappointments, it was about the fact that I made you proud.

It was Not just about what I learned, it was about what you tried to teach me.

It was Not just about the jokes, it was about how we laughed when you told them.

It was Not just about how you could cut, curl and perm, it was about how you preached, prayed and pastored.

It was Not just about my name (Adrain Van) it was about me being you namesake (Albert Van).

It was Not just about how you died, it was about how you lived.

It was Not just about you being my Daddy, it was about you being my Father.

Love,
Adrain Van "Casey" Nolley

Tributes to Pastor Fisher

Then there was two words he constantly said, "Thank you." Whether small or great. So I say thank you Pastor for your leadership and love throughout the years.

My Pastor's Faithfulness to the Church and Love for the Members and Others

My pastor dedicated fifty years of service to the Salem Missionary Baptist Church on 3400 Mitchell Blvd., Fort Worth, Texas 76105.

Daily he would go to the church, stroll across the parking lot, wearing his suit and Stacey Adams shoes. It almost seem he had an "ump" to his walk. Enter into the sanctuary, kneel at the altar and pray. He believed in the power of prayer. Always saying, "Prayer changes things, situations in one's life." His favorite saying, "I have good news. Jesus told me to tell you, 'He's still alive and in the blessing business.'"

In his humor, he would say, "Some things I just don't understand. I don't understand how a black cow can eat green grass and give white milk. I just don't understand. But what I do understand, letters make words and words make a sentence and sentences tell the story."

Fifty years of preaching the gospel, reading the scriptures about our Lord and Savior Jesus Christ. His death, burial and resurrection. Anytime Pastor spoke about letters, words, sentences, he was telling the story about Jesus Christ (BIBLE). Many came through the Salem Church and gave their life to Christ under his leadership. He laid a solid foundation for anyone who came through the doors of Salem and accepted Jesus Christ as their Lord and Savior. His preaching and teaching have not been in vain.

Scriptures I heard him quote for many years. I call them his favorite scriptures, Psalms 23, 103, 116, 121, 122 and St Matthew 7:7, 5:42, 6:33. There were many others but none quoted as often.

Favorite song: I don't know who Jesus is to you, but I know what He is to me. Song always by the (deceased) Lerlee Simmons.

Pastor's love for his members is incomparable. He knew each one by their name, what family line each belongs to. Always greeted everyone with a hug. Attended and preached funerals near and far. Always there to support his members. What a joy to look up and see his smiling face. Always telling us what was right and wrong through scriptures. Correcting us when we were out of order. Still with his arms stretched wide open, saying, "Give me a hug."

And just as he loved his members, he loved others the same way. Many times people came to the church for help, and not one time did Pastor turn them away. But he would ask them to stay for Bible study or to hear the word of God preached. Telling us always to love others regardless of their motives. He would always say, "Just because you are nice to people, people don't have to be nice to you."

To Rev. A.V. Fisher
 This is a letter of expression and appreciation to tell you

how I love you as a man of God. You have been very inspirational in my life. You have depicted in your life how a true Christian should feel and live toward the Creator and have demonstrated how you love the Lord our God and His precious gift to mankind, His only begotten son Jesus.

During your lifetime as my pastor at Salem Church, you have preached to our congregation how to live holy according to God's Word. I want you to know I've enjoyed your jokes and stories. They were very humorous and brought joy to my soul. They illustrated what you were explaining. Yes, Rev. Fisher, you are and have made it very clear to all who have heard you and are willing to incline their ears to what you are saying. You have lived and preached about Christian personality in the fruit of the spirit: joy, peace, patience, kindness, goodness, faithfulness, gentleness and self-control.

As my Pastor, you are, in my opinion, one of God's greatest shepherds and are leading His sheep in what they need.

From one of your sheep,
Sis Mildred Sims

Deacon Archie Prince

Rev. A.V. Fisher is a good friend. Rev. A.V. Fisher is a good man. A good man will be with you until the end. Reverend will pray with you, for you and will be there for you. Rev. Fisher has a giving heart. He will give you his last dime, and as being a deacon of the church, he gives me good advice on how to improve my role in being a deacon. He preached to the congregation of the church to love one another and be on one accord.

Rev. A.V. Fisher is a man of the seven He's:

1. He preaches
2. He teaches
3. He is faithful
4. He tithes
5. He gives offering
6. He prays
7. He loves

A good man ordered by the footsteps of the Lord.

Remembering my Neighbor and Friend

I believe that each person is given the gift of time on this earth; to live... to love... and to leave a legacy.

Our houses were about 75 feet apart. Rev. Fisher was a good neighbor and friend. He was there whenever I needed him.

He was not only a neighbor to me but to all that he came in contact with. For you see a neighbor is one who has no boundaries when needs arise. He was always willing to help somebody. People that he knew or that he did not know. Proverbs 17:17 says, "A friend loveth at all times, and a brother is born for adversity."

Pastor Fisher was a humorist. He tried to bring cheer to the broken hearted with his jokes. He loved to see the smiles and hear the laughter of the people.

Pastor Fisher had many friends and sons in the ministry. He preached in 48 states. Proverbs 18:24 says, "A man that hath friends must show himself friendly: and there is a friend that sticketh closer than a brother."

I was blessed to have Rev. Fisher as my pastor at the Salem Missionary Baptist Church. He showed no envy or jealousy, and he always gave me an opportunity to exercise my gift.

The type of pastor that he was due in part to the integrity of his wife and the discipline of his children. Proverbs 31:23, 28 says, "Her husband is known in the gates, when he sitteth among the elders of the land. Her children arise up, and call her blessed; her husband also, and he praised her."

Pastor Fisher seized every opportunity to bring the lost to Christ. Whether at funerals or other church engagements. He would simply say come: C – children can come. O – old folks can come. M – middle age can come. And E – everybody can come.

Pastor A. V. Fisher's legacy will remain indelibly impressed in the hearts of many who knew him.

Rev. Odis Darnell

Resolutions for Rev. Fisher

    First giving honor to my Lord and Savior Jesus Christ (to great Angel of this Church). To all the ministers on Roster. To this Beautiful Family in Your time of sorrow. To all my brothers and sisters in Christ.

    On Oct 3, 2017, we were so saddened to hear that Pastor A.V. Fisher went home to be with Lord. I can truly say that Pastor Fisher was a Christian man.

    Not only did he preach the Word, he taught the Word and he lived by the Word. Pastor Fisher was Pastor, a friend, a daddy, grandfather, uncle, and a brother. Pastor was just a good person all the way. He had a big heart, he loved everybody. And he was a caring person.

    We the member of Bright Glory Baptist love Pastor Fisher and his family. If there is anything we can do please reach out to us. We will do what we can.

Pastor Charles Irvoy

I say to this family, Pastor Fisher has lived his life. He left a beautiful legacy. So cherish it because it is a beautiful one to live by. So I say to this Family, look to Hills from which cometh all our help. We love you Sis Fisher and the Rest of Family.

Humbly Submitted
Bright Glory Baptist Church

East Fort Interdenominational Ministerial Alliance

Since it has pleased the Almighty God to call our beloved brother closer to Him and enjoy the fruits of eternal living. We know that God never makes a mistake. We understand that our beloved brother will not have any more suffering. In addition, He will have no more pain. We join hands with you to celebrate the life of our beloved brother. According to His tender mercy God, who is infinite in wisdom, has seen fit to move from our midst our beloved brother by means of death on October 3, 2017.

We rejoice for many reasons over our dear brother:
WHEREAS, Pastor A.V. Fisher was one of the founding fathers of the East Fort Worth Interdenominational Ministerial Alliance.
WHEREAS, our dear brother wrote the Alliance constitution many years ago and is still active today!
WHEREAS, Pastor A.V. fisher served in many officer roles in the Alliance. Fisher was Vice President, Treasurer and Secretary.
WHEREAS, Pastor Fisher helped to establish the Annual Banquet and the Annual Revival.
WHEREAS, Pastor A.V. Fisher was instrumental in many preachers' ministries.

WHEREAS, we believe the words of Jesus in John 14 that encourages us to "Let not your heart be troubled; ye believe in God believe also in me. In my father's house are many mansions if it was not so I would have told you. I go to prepare a place for you. And if I go and prepare a place for you, I will come again, and receive you unto myself, that where I am ye may be also."

We Pray May the Peace of God Rest Rule and Abide with You!
Pastor D.C. Jackson President
Rev. Leon A. Brumfield Secretary

Mount Zion First Baptist Church
Resolution of Respect for Pastor Emeritus A.V. Fisher

He's in a better place now
Than he's ever been before;
All pain is gone; he's now at rest.
Nothing trouble him anymore
It's us who feel the burden of
Our sadness and our grief;
We have to cry, to mourn our loss,
Before we can move on
We know we'll connect with him
At the end of each life's road
We'll see his cherished face again
When we release our earthly load.

Pastor Demotis Sherman, Jr. and the Mount Zion First Baptist Church want the Fisher and extended family to know that our hearts are with you as you bid a Christian good-bye to this faithful Sheppard.

We pause here today to express the appreciation of Pastor A.V. Fisher, for he loved God, life and family. He was faithful in preaching the Word of God and would say rejoice in the Lord for joy will come in the morning.

> Why do we mourn departed love ones?
> Or shake at death's alarm,
> This is but the voice that Jesus sends
> To call them to his arms.
> Another faithful soldier gone.
> To get his great reward
> He fought the good fight, and kept the faith
> And now he's gone home --- HOME TO GOD.

Whereas, the passing of Pastor Fisher is the will of God, and there is a human tie that has been broken, which bleeds the heart in agony and pain. We are encouraged and consoled in the words: "Let not your heart be troubled, in my father's house are many mansions; if it were not so I would have told you. And if I go and prepare a place for you, I will come again, and receive you unto myself; that where I am, there ye may be also." John 14:1-3

Therefore be it resolved, that we embrace the family to show our love and support in this time of sorrow. We cannot replace Pastor Fisher, but we can demonstrate our love by trying to be there if you need us.

Be it further resolved that a copy of this resolution be given to the family and a copy placed in the church archives of Salem Missionary Baptist Church and Mount Zion First Baptist Church.

Humbly submitted on this 11th day of October 2017.
Rev. Demotis Sherman, Jr.
Sis. Jackie Reed - Administrative Assistant
520 Stafford Street
Mount Zion First Baptist Church
Abilene, Texas 79601

The Reaching Out To You Ministry
Sixth Ave. Baptist Church ~125 S. 5th St. Corsicana, Texas 75110
Overseer/Bishop K.D. Davis, Sr. Pastor

To: The Family of Pastor A.V. Fisher

This is the day that the Lord has made. Let us rejoice and be glad in it. II Corinthians 5:1-10 states, "For we know that if the earthly house of our tabernacle be dissolved, we have a building from God, a house not made with hands, eternal, in the heavens."

Whereas, in the providence of God, He has brought to a close, the life of Pastor A.V. Fisher, Bishop K.D. Davis, Sr., the officers and members of the Sixth Ave Baptist Church extend our heartfelt sympathy to the Fisher Family. We want you to know that we love you and are praying for you and your family.

We are placed in this world for a limited time. And with the breath of the infant, begins the race to the grave. A race that everyone must run. The gray head is a crown of glory, it shall be found in the way of the righteous. (Proverbs 16:31).

It is our prayer to God that you find comfort in each loving memory of Pastor Fisher and peace through your faith in an all-wise and all-mighty God. Earth has no sorrow that Heaven cannot heal. We know that all things work together for the good of them that love the Lord and are called according to His purpose.

Be it therefore resolved that we bow in humble submission to Him who never makes a mistake and remind the family to be encouraged, with this scripture.

"Trust in The Lord with all thine heart and lean not unto thine own understanding; in all thy ways acknowledge Him and He shall direct thy paths. (Proverbs 3:5-6).

Prayerfully Submitted,

This eleventh day of October in the year of our Lord two thousand and seventeen.

Mount Olive Missionary Baptist Church
October 11, 2017
Fort Worth, Texas 76104

"He that dwelleth in the secret place of the most High shall abide under the shadow of the Almighty. I will say of the Lord, He is my refuge and my fortress: my God; in him will I trust. He shall call upon me, and I will answer him: I will be with him in trouble; I will deliver him, and honor him. With long life will I satisfy him, and shew him my salvation." (Psalm 91:1, 2, 15 and 16)

We, the officers and members of the Mount Olive Missionary Baptist Church, wish to express our love and compassion at the passing of your loved one, Revered Albert V. Fisher. We give recognition to those family members who are faithful members of the Mount Olive Church Family, we love you.

Reverend Fisher was a true Servant of the Lord, having

accepted his calling to the ministry and serving as a Pastor for approximately fifty (50) years. He willingly taught and preached God's Word when and wherever opportunities were presented.

He was serious about the salvation of those he met and would frequently check in with family and friends to encourage them to stay faithful to the lord. He was active in church related activities, attending local and national conventions.

Reverend Fisher was also active in the community, he supported and participated in political campaigns and City Council issues. He was a member of the NAACP. He was an entrepreneur with a successful Barber and Beauty Shop where he also worked for approximately fifty (50) years. He was honored with a Business Owner of the Year Award.

Reverend Fisher loved his mother, wife and family; he was a stable, loving and hard-working family man. He enjoyed spending time with family and always attended Family Reunions, birthday and wedding celebrations as well as funerals. He was a frequent traveler to Marshall, Texas to share with family; he encouraged the family to stay together.

Reverend Fisher was truly a people person, he was friendly, outgoing, and had a beautiful, contagious smile with a gregarious personality. He was always ready to share a joke with all he met. During leisure time, he relaxed with his favorite game and comedy shows; his cell phone was well used, and he liked to play table games, and snow cones were one of his favorite snacks. He enjoyed reading and keeping up with the news in the Evangelical magazine, ERRP.

Reverend Fisher was blessed to live a long, productive life. He will be truly missed. He labored long, he fought a good fight. Heaven is a prepared place for prepared people. Reverend

Fisher was prepared. We encourage you to find comfort in the happy memories you shared with Reverend Fisher as a family member or friend. Our prayer is that you will find peace in knowing that God will not forsake you or leave you. He will guide and sustain you in the coming days, continue to lean and depend on Him.

Humbly submitted,
The Mount Olive Missionary Baptist Church
Reverend William T. Glynn, Pastor

ACKNOWLEDGEMENT

To The Loving Family of Pastor Albert Van Fisher:

We send you our thoughts and lift you up in prayers. Please remember The Lord loves you and He cares. A few words from our hearts cannot fully express the love of the Good Lord's tenderness.

During sunshine or rain, if you trust the Lord, He shall remove the pain. Jesus promised He shall never leave you. Yes faith in The Lord requires complete trust.

In John Chapter 11 verse 25, Jesus said, "I am the resurrection and the life." It is wonderful to know, in Jesus there is everlasting life!

The International Bishops Conference & Ministers Fellowship, Incorporated
Bishop Dr. Rickey Moore Sr. Presiding Prelate,
Bishop Collier Banks 1st Presiding Prelate,
Bishop Jones 2nd Presiding Prelate, and

Bishop Dr. LaMark Carver Secretary

**New harvest Missionary Baptist Church
RESOLUTION
In Loving Memory of Pastor A.V. Fisher**

On behalf of the bereaved family of Pastor A.V. Fisher, the church family of New Harvest Missionary Baptist Church wants you to know that we sincerely share the deep sorrow you are experiencing at the home-going of your loved one, and we extend our deepest sympathy and condolences to you and to the many friends gathered here today.

Although we never like saying goodbye to those we love, there is no need to despair — for we have the assurance that once with the Lord, all sickness, pain, suffering, trials and tribulations will be no more.

So we say to the family, be strong and of good courage and lean upon the everlasting arms of Jesus. May He strengthen each of you and give you all His abiding love and peace is our prayer.

Humbly submitted on this 11th day of October, 2017.

Dr. Clyde Downs, Senior Pastor

**RESOLUTION
To the family of
Pastor Albert Van Fisher**

"It is appointed unto man once to die but after this, the judgment; so Christ was once offered to bear the sins of many;

and unto them that look for Him shall He appear the second time without sin unto salvation." (Hebrews 9:27-28)

Death is a door provided by a loving father, by which his children are granted preserved passage from an earthly existence into an eternal habitation. It is the divine journey by which the weary travel down the roads of life and gains relief from the cares of this world.

For the Word of the Lord affirms, "If our earthly house of this tabernacle were dissolved, we have a building of God, a house not made with hands, eternal in the heavens." (2 Corinthians 5:1)

Be it resolved that Senior Pastor Darrell W. Blair and the members of New Breed Christian Center bow in humble submission to the divine purpose and providence of God, being fully aware that death is but a transitory moment, and through it comes eternal life. It is the avenue by which the believer rids themselves of the garment of mortality and is clothed with a glorified garment, divinely tailored by the hand of God.

New Breed Christian Center offers our continued prayers, love, support, and encouragement, to our beloved member, Sister Brittany Stevenson and to the host of family, friends and loved ones of Pastor Albert Van Fisher, our heartfelt sympathies.

"Hast thou not known? Hast thou not heard? That the everlasting God, the LORD, the Creator of the ends of the earth, fainteth not, neither is weary? There is no searching of his understanding. He giveth power to the faint; and to them that have no might he increaseth strength. Even the youths shall faint and be weary, and the young men shall utterly fall: But they that wait upon the LORD shall renew their strength;

they shall mount up with wings as eagles; they shall run, and not be weary; and they shall walk, and not faint." (Isaiah 40:28-31) May you be comforted in knowing that "Earth has no sorrow that Heaven cannot heal."

"Now unto Him that is able to keep you from falling, and to present you faultless before the presence of His glory with exceeding joy, to the only wise God our Savior, be glory and majesty, dominion and power both now and forever, Amen." (Jude 1:24-25)

Lovingly, and tenderly submitted this 11th day of October in the year of our Lord 2017, by the New Breed Christian Center, 4500 S. Riverside Drive, Fort Worth, TX 76119.
Pastor Darrell W. Blair, Senior Pastor

Editor/Publisher's Note:
From Lisa Bell, Radical Women
To the Family and Friends of Pastor Fisher

I met Verdell Fisher in the fall of 2017. I never had the privilege of knowing her beloved husband. Yet through this project, I came to know a man of God's Word who deeply loved his family and the members of his church and the entire body of Christ.

I pray that the words captured in this book fulfill his dream, which Mrs. Fisher so diligently pursued after his passing. May we all live the legacy left behind by this godly pastor who wanted more than anything to honor our Lord and Savior, Jesus Christ.

Lisa Bell, Author, Editor, Publisher

About the Author

A.V. Fisher was the sixth child of seven children born to Essie J. and Corine Caraway Fisher on April 21, 1933 in Marshall (Harrison County) Texas. He attended Oakhill Elementary School, New Town Elementary and graduated from Pemberton High School. After graduation he attended Tyler Barber College and went on to become the first male to complete Cosmetology from Valarie Hurd Beauty College. He cut hair at Leffall Barber Shop and gave many haircuts to many outstanding football players. A.V. served in the army. Reverend Dr. A.V. Fisher was definitely a trailblazer in his area of expertise.

Dr. Fisher perfected his craft by moving to Fort Worth, Teas in 1958 and opened his first beauty salon on 4th Street. The shop began to grow and had to relocate to Elmwood Street and now the present location at 2909 Evans Avenue. He was featured in *Ebony and Beauty Trade Magazines* as one of the top 100 beauty operators in the United States. The Texas Legislature and the Texas State Association and Beauty Culturist League #47 honored him for 50 years as a hair stylist and salon owner.

He met the love of his life, Verdell Knighten and they married in 1957. They had four children, Londell (Skip), Avis Michelle, Ava LaNell and Adrain Van (Casey). Verdell took the information A.V. Fisher compiled and worked to finish the book project he began.

In 1963 Pastor Fisher answered the call into the

Gospel Ministry, preaching his first sermon on Mother's Day under the spiritual guidance of Reverend James Warren and Dr. M.R. Lester. In 1968 Pastor Fisher became the pastor of the Salem Missionary Baptist Church after the demise of Reverend J.T. Robinson. During his tenure as pastor, Reverend Fisher has taken in hundreds of people for Kingdom Building, baptized many, ordained over 300 deacons and installed over 200 preachers as pastors all over the United States, performed numerous weddings and conducted many funerals.

For over 30 years, Pastor Fisher was the coordinator for the Martin Luther King Jr. Memorial Service and Prayer Breakfast, Treasurer, Vice-President and President of the Baptist Minister's Union; President of the IMA and Founder of the Black Pastor's Association; one of the founding fathers of the East Fort Worth Interdenominational Ministerial Alliance in which he wrote the constitution; 1st Vice-President of the Central Missionary Baptist General Convention of Texas; Moderator of the Original Harmony District Association; in 1977 Pastor Fisher founded the Evangelical Report Religious Magazine. This magazine provides national religious news coverage for pastors and non-pastors. He also graduated from the New World Bible Institute, has received numerous awards, an honorary doctorate and has traveled and preached all across the US and the Bahamas.

Pastor Fisher fought a good fight; he kept the faith and heard God say "Well done my good and faithful servant" at the age of 84 on Tuesday, October 3, 2017.

"I am excited and delighted. I've got good news for you. Jesus told me to tell you He is still alive and in the blessing business. I will bless the Lord at all times. His praise shall continue to be in my mouth." Pastor Fisher embodied these words, and lived his life based on them for himself and as a role model for others.

Well done, good and faithful servant.

www.ingramcontent.com/pod-product-compliance
Lightning Source LLC
Chambersburg PA
CBHW051036160426
43193CB00010B/966